THIRTY
Monologues and Duologues for South Asian Actors

THIRTY
Monologues and Duologues for South Asian Actors

Celebrating 30 Years of Kali Theatre's
South Asian Women Playwrights

Extracts from plays produced by Kali 1991–2021

Edited by Helena Bell

Assisted by Christopher Corner and Naomi Joseph

Selection panel: Rukhsana Ahmad, Helena Bell, Penny Gold,
Trilby James, Naomi Joseph, Janet Steel

methuen | drama
LONDON • NEW YORK • OXFORD • NEW DELHI • SYDNEY

METHUEN DRAMA

Bloomsbury Publishing Plc

50 Bedford Square, London, WC1B 3DP, UK

1385 Broadway, New York, NY 10018, USA

29 Earlsfort Terrace, Dublin 2, Ireland

BLOOMSBURY, METHUEN DRAMA and the Methuen Drama logo are
trademarks of Bloomsbury Publishing Plc

First published in Great Britain 2021

Cover design: Rebecca Heselton
Cover image © Ikin Yum

A catalogue record for this book is available from the British Library.

A catalog record for this book is available from the Library of Congress.

ISBN: PB: 978-1-3502-0389-1
        ePDF: 978-1-3502-0390-7
        eBook: 978-1-3502-0391-4

Series: Audition Speeches, 49

Typeset by RefineCatch Limited, Bungay, Suffolk
Printed and bound in Great Britain

To find out more about our authors and books visit www.bloomsbury.com
and sign up for our newsletters.

Contents

Foreword

Rukhsana Ahmad, Artistic Director 1991–2002

Founding Kali Theatre Company was a brave plan. Born in a moment of gritty determination that followed a wild DIY impulse, it was a challenge for us novices. Rita Wolf, my Co-Artistic Director until the end of 1992, recounts the story of our first production on Kali's website. Had it not been for a last-minute loan from Rita's father, we would have had to hide from our debtors . . .

As co-founders, we were lucky to have supportive friends and family, and, later, benefactors amongst funders. One of our Arts Council England officers often admitted that the greatest subsidy to theatre comes from practitioners. We certainly got that from many fellow creatives. At the heart of theatre is a genuine spirit of collaboration and trust; something we've all held sacred at Kali.

From those early years of self-exploitation and struggle began a company that has bedded in powerfully. It has served so many women, over so many years, so successfully that it should be cited as a model for inclusion and diversity. What we sought was not some kind of ethnic apartheid from the mainstream but simply the right to programme the stories that mattered to us and reflected our lives. This book illustrates the achievement of that goal.

The secret behind our commendable record of highly original productions and readings has been the professionalism of our artistic directors and their commitment to our writing community from the outset. Janet Steel gave us a steady lead for over fourteen years after Rita and I left Kali. And now, Helena Bell has taken over with equal panache and tremendous passion. At its core, is our dedicated all-women board. Their unerring steer, which gives space to the artistic director and the team without losing sight of Kali's goals and objectives, has provided stability and vision. Thank you, Janet, for raising us to maturity. I loved the coming-of-age party back then. Thank you, Helena, for forging ahead, and for conceiving and organising this brilliant publication.

Thirty years on, it's a humbling experience for me to see a monologue from my play *River on Fire* open this anthology and a duologue from my last one close it. In between, there's so much to celebrate, to be proud of and to reiterate: the choicest cuts from scores of our brilliant productions. It's a tribute to our wonderful writers: those who are here and those to come.

Let me conclude with a timely call from my co-founder, Rita Wolf: 'From a loan to get our first play up and running to twenty-three shows and counting. Kali was very necessary back then and is very, very necessary now. Keep writing!'

Foreword

Janet Steel, Artistic Director 2002–2016

I had the enormous pleasure of working with seventeen of the twenty-two talented writers included in this collection. Reading the scripts again took me straight back to the rehearsal rooms, the theatres and the many train carriages we travelled in on our tours around the UK. I could hear the actors' voices, see their movements, feel the audience's reactions, and remember being told to pipe down as we chatted and laughed too loudly in the quiet coaches.

Each play had its unique journey, the actors, stage managers, creatives, Kali team and directors were all there to collaboratively bring the writer's world and characters to life. There were many discussions and sometimes debates, but the struggle was a part of the process and a reflection of the passion we felt, and the shared desire to be brave and truthful.

The Kali writers wrote stories that mattered to them, which culturally diverse audiences around the country identified with or grappled with. The plays explored a range of themes including family dynamics, addiction, mental health, first love, immigration, poverty and geopolitics. They were stories about men and women, who, as most people do at some point in their life, experienced conflict, loss, regret. There was also plenty of humour, sometimes dark or absurd, from sharp-tongued characters, all played by brilliant actors.

I do hope that readers of these monologues and duologues are inspired to look at the complete play texts they come from, and companies and theatres are motivated to produce them. They are not stories from the past to be produced only once, they are stories of the present that are crying out to be heard again and again.

Foreword

Helena Bell, Artistic Director from 2016

This book is about celebration! THIRTY is here to celebrate Kali's thirtieth birthday, showcasing thirty extracts from a dazzling array of plays by our writers. The book is also here to celebrate the actors, directors, dramaturges and theatre teams who collaborated on these scripts, enabling them to reach their full potential in productions. It is to say thank you to our audiences and funders. All those who have believed in the company's mission and the vital need for these intrepid plays by fearless women to be seen and heard.

As well as celebrating Kali's history and legacy, THIRTY is also an active manual for South Asian actors looking for juicy audition roles. There is so much variety to choose from with characters ranging in age from sixteen to seventy; roles for both women and men to play all classes from all religious faiths (and none). Locations span Afghanistan, India and Pakistan to Europe and the UK. Time frames range from the contemporary to period drama set during the Second World War. You can purchase the complete plays from our Script Shop via the Kali website.

THIRTY is equally intended for literary managers and directors looking for an accomplished writer to commission. Short writer biographies can be found at the back of this book. Kali continues to champion and showcase established playwrights through our FESTIVAL Programme – a loosely themed biennial festival of staged readings of new plays.

To all you aspiring playwrights – Kali is here for you too and we hope you'll find this collection a source of inspiration and encouragement. Check out our national DISCOVERY programme which develops and showcases twelve talented women writers in each new intake. We look forward to welcoming you.

Finally I'd like to celebrate and thank my brilliant team at Kali – Chris and Naomi and our wonderful board alongside the superb selection panel for this book, all of whom have been instrumental in Kali's development. Special thanks must also go to Trilby James for her expert advice on audition books.

Happy Birthday, Kali! Thank you, Rukhsana, Janet and all who have given Kali life and light.

Intrepid plays by fearless women since 1991

Kali Theatre develops and presents ground-breaking, thought-provoking, contemporary theatre by women writers of South Asian descent that reflects and comments on our lives today.

We seek out and nurture talented writers, bringing their experience and stories to audiences from all backgrounds to transform the theatre landscape and better reflect the diversity of modern Britain.

Our annual programme includes writer development seasons each spring (Discovery/ Festival) and a national touring production of a new play each autumn.   Most of our new play commissions will undergo Kali's rigorous script development programme before they reach the stage, ensuring quality and excellence.

Kali's writers, actors and creative teams have won numerous awards and accolades throughout our thirty years.   Landmark productions include *Song for a Sanctuary* (1991), *River on Fire* (2000/1), *Calcutta Kosher* (2004/2012), *Zameen* (2008), *Behna* (2011), *Mustafa* (2012), *The Dishonoured* (2016), *Sundowning* (2018), *Homing Birds* (2019) and *The Last Clap* (2020).

Kali is proud to champion so many talented writers and actors, significantly contributing to a more diverse entertainment industry. We are delighted to see British television, film and radio alongside our national theatres becoming more culturally diverse with the increasing presence of our South Asian artists.   We look forward to continuing our talent development and introducing Kali's distinct perspective and inspiring new work to audiences and industry everywhere.

Find out more at www.kalitheatre.co.uk

Artistic Director	Helena Bell
Executive Director	Christopher Corner
Administrator	Naomi Joseph
Artistic Associates	Poonam Brah, Pooja Ghai, Aileen Gonsalves
Board Chair	Alison McFadyen
Board Members	Rukhsana Ahmad, Elizabeth Cuffy, Penny Gold, Shelley King, Shivani Mathur, Nigham Shahid, Shiroma Silva, Jocelyn Watson, Kithmini Wimalasekera

Kali wishes to thank: Komal Amin, Tim Collingridge, the late Tony Craze (founding Chair), Samia Djilli, Robert Day, Tim Dukes, Cheryl Gallacher, Trina Haldar, Isobel Hawson, Jo Hemmant, Natasha Kathi-Chandra, Preethi Manuel, Nancy Poole, David Prescott, Jessica Thanki, Pam Vision, Luke Wakeman, Binita Walia, Rita Wolf, Robert Workman, Kamila Zahno.

Kali is a resident company at The Albany in Deptford

Kali is an Arts Council England National Portfolio Organisation

Productions 1991–2021

1991 *Song for a Sanctuary* by Rukhsana Ahmad*
Inspired by the true story of a Sikh woman murdered by her husband inside a refuge, the play is an exploration of conflicting tensions between women in the refuge.
Director Rita Wolf   **Designer** Carla Eve Aimie
Lighting Alison Wheeler.
Cast Kusum Haider, Jackie Cowper, Sayan Akaddas, Susan McGoun, Sanny Bharti, Simon Nagra
Venues Lyric Hammersmith
Autumn tour: **Directors** Rita Wolf and Sue Parrish.
Cast Joanna Bacon, Sanny Bharti, Jackie Cowper, Jamila Massey, Simon Nagra, Rita Wolf.
Venues Birmingham Rep Studio & short tour
First Performance 7 October 1991
This followed an earlier reading of the play at Riverside Studios

1997 *Natural World* by Joyoti Grech
The story follows a father and daughter as they embark on a journey of love, loss and individual identity.
Director Anne Edyvean   **Designer** Carla Evie Aimie
Lighting Crin Claxton
Cast Nathalie Armin, Ravin Ganatra, Nina Wadia
Venues Ovalhouse, Tara Studio, Leicester Haymarket and a short tour
First Performance 20 February 1997

1999 *The Ecstasy* by Anu Kumar Lazarus*
The play depicts the relationship between a sculptor, his model and his boyfriend. It deals with themes of love, friendship and homosexuality.
& *Black Shalwar* by Rukhsana Ahmad (adapted from a short story by Manto). Evoking the epic romanticism of pre-Partition India, Black Shalwar is a smouldering tale about Sultana, a feisty prostitute who falls in love and starts to lose her grip on reality.
Director Helena Bell   **Designer** Sophia Lovell Smith
Lighting David Lawrence
Cast Ashvin Kumar Joshi, Adele Salem, Royce Ullah
Venues Ovalhouse, Brentford Watermans & UK tour
First Performance 4 March 1999
Produced under the joint title of *Love Comes in at the Window*

2000   *River on Fire* by Rukhsana Ahmad*
–2001   Set against the Bombay riots of December 1992, this is a
contemporary re-working of the ancient myth of Antigone. A
young actress's life is thrown into turmoil when tragedy strikes
and she is forced to grapple with communalism.
Director Helena Bell **Designer** Sophia Lovell Smith
Lighting Flick Ansell
Lyric Hammersmith Cast Ravi Aujla, Lyndam Gregory, Shiv
Grewal, Shelley King, Parminder K. Nagra, Parminder Sekhon
Touring Cast Ravi Aujla, Sumitra Bhagat, Lyndam Gregory,
Shelley King, Rina Mahoney, Sanjit Sil
Venues Lyric Hammersmith, Leicester Haymarket & UK tour
First Performance 31 October 2000
Finalist, Susan Smith Blackburn International Award

2002   *Singh Tangos* by Bettina Gracias*
Mrs Singh has discovered the liberating effect of dancing, much
to her family's embarrassment. A sparkling comedy that playfully
examines integration, modernity and tradition.
Director Caroline Ward
Designer David Blight   **Lighting** Douglas Kuhrt
Music Troy Banarzi
Cast Siddiqua Akhtar, Imran Ali, Pooja Ghai, Kaleem Janjua
Venues Riverside Studios, Derby Playhouse, Leicester
Haymarket & UK tour
First Performance 25 April 2002

2003   *Sock 'em with Honey* by Bapsi Sidhwa
Tensions arise in a Parsi family when their daughter falls in love
with a Jewish American man. A bittersweet comedy about love,
loyalties, intercultural relationships and the need to belong.
Director Janet Steel   **Designer** Penny White
Music Sayan Kent
Cast Sumitra Bhagat, Gareth Clarke, Norma Dixit, Philippa
Downes, Kitu Gidwani, Rohit Gokani
Venues Cockpit Theatre, Leicester Haymarket & UK tour
First Performance 20 March 2003

2004   *Calcutta Kosher* by Shelley Silas*
Set in the Indian Jewish community of Calcutta, two sisters are
forced to come to terms with their mother's secret history. This
funny and moving play examines how family and culture, time
and distance influence our sense of who we are.
Director Janet Steel
Designer Magdalen Rubalcava   **Lighting** Flick Ansell

Music Sayan Kent
Cast Seema Bowri, Shelley King, Jamila Massey, Richard Santhiri,
Harvey Virdi
Venues Southwark Playhouse & UK tour
Co-production with Tara Arts
First Performance 4 February 2004
In June 2004 this production was presented by Theatre Royal
Stratford East

2005 *Bells* by Yasmin Whittaker-Khan*
A glimpse into the seedy world of Mujra (courtesan) clubs, a
centuries-old Pakistani tradition spread underground in the UK,
Bells pierces the glitz and glamour to expose the pain and
degradation of secret lives.
Director Poonam Brah
Cast Damien Asher, Marc Elliot, Shivani Ghai, Nicholas Khan,
Sharona Sassoon.
& *Chaos* by Azma Dar*
A man's ambitions to become a local councillor are thrown into
turmoil as his family reveals shocking secrets and world events
spiral out of control. A dark, frantic comedy about the collapse
of personal and political understanding and the disastrous
consequences which follow.
Director Janet Steel
Cast Damian Asher, Marc Elliot, Nicholas Khan, Shelley King,
Jamila Massey
Designer Matthew Wright   **Lighting** Chris Corner
Music Sayan Kent
Venues Southwark Playhouse, Birmingham Repertory Theatre &
UK tour
Chaos **First Performance** 16 March   *Bells* **First Performance**
23 March

2006 *Paper Thin* by Azma Dar*
A fresh and unconventional look at the complexities of
immigration. A desperate student wants an arranged marriage of
convenience in order to stay in London.
Director Janet Steel   **Designer** Matthew Wright
Lighting Philip Gladwell   **Music** Sayan Kent
Cast Pushpinder Chani, Shelley King, Alan Suri, Joan Walker
Venues Brentford Watermans Arts & UK tour
Originally co-commissioned by Watermans & Theatre Royal
Stratford East
First Performance 22 February 2006

2006   *Deadeye* by Amber Lone*
A gritty, contemporary drama exploring second-generation struggles and exposing the misunderstandings and hypocrisies that divide the generations.
Director Janet Steel
Designer Matthew Wright   **Lighting** Simon Bond
Music Sayan Kent
Cast Shane Zaza, Chetna Pandya, Sakuntala Ramanee, Madhav Sharma, Pushpinder Chani, Beth Vyse
Venues Birmingham Repertory Theatre, Soho Theatre, Nottingham Lakeside, Manchester.
Contact Co-production with Birmingham Repertory Theatre & Soho Theatre
First Performance 12 October 2006

2007   *A Thin Red Line* by Sonali Bhattacharyya*
A young couple return home to confront the fault lines of prejudice and cultural division that had driven them to find sanctuary just a few miles away.
Director Janet Steel
Cast Pushpinder Chani, Rebecca Clarke, Gregg Hobbs, Bharti Patel
Venues Soho Theatre, Birmingham Repertory Theatre & community venues in the Black Country
Co-production with Black Country Touring & Birmingham Repertory Theatre
First Performance 7 November 2007

2008   *Zameen* by Satinder Chohan*
In the cotton fields of Punjab, an ageing farmer grapples with the rapidly changing nature of agriculture as a result of globalisation, while his children romanticise prosperous lives abroad.
Director Janet Steel
Designer Emma Wee   **Lighting** Jenny Cane   **Music** Sayan Kent
Cast Bhasker Patel, Goldy Notay, Ravin J. Ganatra, Gurpreet Singh, Amarjit Bassan
Venues Arts Theatre, Manchester Contact, Leeds Playhouse & UK tour
First Performance 23 April 2008

2009   *Another Paradise* by Sayan Kent*
Set in a world in the not so distant future, when identity cards are compulsory and people are validated only by their digital ID, five people's lives are thrown into confusion when their official identities vanish with surprising and hilarious results.

Director Janet Steel
Designer Alice Hoult   **Lighting** Chris Corner
Music Sayan Kent
Cast Shelley King, Karen Mann, Chand Martinez, Sarah Paul, Richard Rees
Venues   Manchester Contact, Vanbrugh Theatre & UK tour
First Performance 12 March 2009

2010   *Behna* by Sonia Likhari*
In this unique, intimate and lively piece of theatre, a family struggles with private jealousies and family secrets in the midst of public weddings, births and separations.
Director Janet Steel
Cast   Sandeep Garcha, Shaleen Hudda, Hema Mangoo, Ansuya Nathan, Simon Nagra
Venues Presented in real kitchens in houses in Birmingham and the Black Country
Co-production with Birmingham Repertory Theatre & Black Country Touring
First Performance 3 March 2010

2010   *Black-i* by Sharon Raizada*
Knife-crime, the pressures of youth and love on the edge are explored in this compelling and unconventional romance at the dark heart of London.
Director Poonam Brah
Designer Alice Hoult   **Lighting** William Reynolds
Music Hamid Selalian
Cast Gina Abolins, Waleed Akhtar, Louise Bangay
Venue Ovalhouse
First Performance 19 October 2010

2010   *Gandhi and Coconuts* by Bettina Gracias*
Frustrated with her dull married life, Asha escapes to the India of her imagination where Mahatma Gandhi and the Hindu gods Shiva and Kali arrive for tea. This witty, playful and poignant play asks if it is better to be sane or happy?
Director Janet Steel
Designer Alice Hoult   **Lighting** Chris Corner
Music James Hesford
Cast Sophiya Haque, Nimmi Harasgama, Rez Kempton, Robert Mountford, Gary Pillai

Venues Arcola Theatre
First Performance 24 November 2010
January 2011 tour to Plymouth Drum, Leicester Curve & The Public, West Bromwich

2011   *Behna* (revival) by Sonia Likhari*
Director Janet Steel
Cast Sandeep Garcha, Shaleen Hudda, Hema Mangoo, Balvinder Sopal, Gurpreet Singh
Venues Presented in real kitchens in houses in Sandwell & West London
Co-production with The Public, West Bromwich & Black Country Touring
First Performance (of revival) 22 March 2011

2012   *Purnjanam/Born Again* by Sharmila Chauhan*
Director Janet Steel
In a city of transition and tradition, three liars, two lovers and a reluctant leader all desperately search for truth. Purnjanam questions destiny, love and power, to ask what must be destroyed for something new to be created.
& *Endless Light* by Sayan Kent*
Director Elizabeth Freestone
An activist protests against an opencast coal mine on top of a sacred mountain. As the situation escalates, the activist and the mine owner discover they share a secret they can no longer avoid.
Designer Molly Einchcomb   **Lighting** Richard Howell
Music Arun Ghosh
Cast Rebecca Grant, Manjeet Mann, Robert Mountford, Goldy Notay, Dharmesh Patel, Gary Pillai
Venue Southwark Playhouse
First Performance 17 January 2012

2012   *Mustafa* by Naylah Ahmed*
Mustafa is in prison for the death of a teenage boy during an exorcism. When prisoners who taunt him suffer mysterious injuries and prison officers start behaving strangely, Mustafa realises the spirit he tried to banish is still with him and he must confront it once more.
Director Janet Steel   **Designer** Colin Falconer
Lighting Tim Mitchell   **Music** Arun Ghosh
Cast Ryan Early, Munir Khairdin, Paul McCleary, Gary Pillai

Venues Soho Theatre, Birmingham Repertory Theatre, Royal
Exchange & UK tour
Co-production with Birmingham Repertory Theatre & Soho Theatre
First Performance 7 March 2012
Four Off West End Theatre Award nominations including for
Best New Play.

2012 *Kabaddi Kabaddi Kabaddi* by Satinder Chohan*
A powerful drama about sport, nationality and belonging, with a
haunting love story at its heart. From the red dust of Punjab to the
Olympic stadiums of Europe this intense drama explores the
Indian sport of Kabaddi and its place on the world stage.
Director Helena Bell
Designer Sophia Lovell Smith   **Lighting** Mark Dymock
Music Arun Ghosh
Cast Pushpinder Chani, Asif Khan, Shalini Peiris
Venues Arcola Theatre & UK tour
First Performance 8 November 2012
Co-production with Pursued by a Bear
National Lottery Awards nomination.

2012 *Calcutta Kosher* (revival for 21st birthday) by Shelley Silas
Director Janet Steel
Designer Alice Hoult   **Lighting** Prema Mehta
Music Sayan Kent
Cast Shelley King, Jane Lowe, Rina Mahoney, Harvey Virdi,
Kaleem Janjua
Venue Arcola Theatre
First Performance 11 December 2012

2013 *My Daughter's Trial* by Gulshanah Choudhuri (Jabine Chaudri)
An ambitious young Muslim barrister struggles with the conflict
between her professional life as a barrister and her family duty as
a daughter.
Director Janet Steel   **Costume** Joseph Marshall
Music Jai Channa
Cast Goldy Notay, Sakuntala Ramanee, Narinder Samra, James
Daniel Wilson, Gordon Cooper, Robin Griffith
Venues Browns Courtrooms & site specific UK tour
First Performance 4 April 2013

2013   *Speed* by Iman Qureshi
In this wry modern comedy, five sexy, sassy and cynical twenty-somethings come together at a less than glamorous speed-dating event.
Director Poonam Brah   **Designer** Alice Hoult
Lighting Prema Mehta
Cast Dina Mousawi, Goldy Notay, Jaz Deol, Tariq Jordan, Divian Ladwa
Venue Tristan Bates Theatre
First Performance 25 February 2013
Revived in 2014 at the same venue with Joanna Burnett, Goldy Notay, Tariq Jordan, Divian Ladwa, Jai Rajani

2014   *The Husbands* by Sharmila Chauhan*
A tale of love and wonder, set in a society where women practise polyandry. A household prepares for a wedding but the arrival of a stranger threatens to challenge everything they believe in.
Director Janet Steel
Designer Jean Chan   **Lighting** Prema Mehta
Music Arun Ghosh
Cast Phillip Edgerley, Syreeta Kumar, Rhik Samadder, Mark Theodore
Venues Soho Theatre, Plymouth Drum & UK tour
Co-production with Pentabus Theatre
First Performance 12 February 2014

2014   *My Big Fat Cowpat Wedding* by Sayan Kent*
A celebration of a mixed marriage between a girl from the country and a boy from the city. What could possibly go wrong?
Directors Janet Steel & Steve Johnstone   **Designer** Abigail King
Cast Aimee Berwick, Sheena Patel, Aaron Virdee, Graeme Rose
Venues Wolverhampton Arts Centre & tour of village halls & community centres
Co-production with Black Country Touring
First Performance 2 October 2014

2015   *Twelve* by Sonali Bhattacharyya, Sharmila Chauhan, Satinder Chohan, Azma Dar, Tanika Gupta, Bettina Gracias, Sayan Kent, Yasmeen Khan, Anu Kumar, Amber Lone, Nessah Muthy & Yasmin Whittaker-Khan
Twelve moving and humorous stories of friendship, first love, defiance, death and survival by twelve different writers, all

inspired by reports of young women murdered by their families in the UK, where on average twelve such killings occur each year.
Director Janet Steel   **Choreography** Sheema Kermani
Set Binita Walia   **Costume** Darien Mynarski
Lighting Chris Corner
Cast Patience James, Sheema Kermani, Maggie O'Brien, Aryana Ramkhalawon, Harvey Virdi, Amina Zia
Venues Brentford Watermans, Birmingham mac & Rich Mix
First Performance 14 April 2015

2016   *She Is Not Herself* by Veronica J. Dewan
Two strangers embark on a journey to confront the injustices of the past, negotiating a minefield of emotions in the process.   An honest and unflinching story of adoption.
Director Helena Bell
Cast Maggie O'Brien, Amina Zia
& *Stateless* by Subika Anwar
Home from serving in Afghanistan, Denny is now the gatekeeper of a psychiatric hospital. But when he receives an unexpected visit from an intriguing stranger, personal story collides with contemporary politics.
Director Trilby James
Cast Simon James Baillie, Shanaya Rafaat
Designer Sophia Lovell Smith **Lighting** Jai Morjaria
Venue Tristan Bates Theatre
First Performance (both plays) 19 January 2016

2016   *The Dishonoured* by Aamina Ahmad*
Set in a world of deceit and violence, espionage and secret agents, this compelling political thriller explores what happens when professional ambition and private life collide.
Director Janet Steel
Designer Anthony Lamble   **Lighting** Prema Mehta
Music Jai Channa
Cast Neil D'Souza, Zaqi Ismail, David Michaels, Robert Mountford, Goldy Notay, Maya Saroya
Venues Arcola Theatre, Leicester Curve & UK tour
First Performance 10 March 2016
Two Off West End Theatre Award nominations – Best New Play & Best Male Performance in a Supporting Role (David Michaels). Winner of the 2019 ScreenCraft Stage Play Competition

2016   *Sweets and Chocolates* by Shazia Ashraf
An exploration of the effects of child abuse on three otherwise unconnected lives which asks questions about the abuse of power and the need to speak the truth.
Director Shona Morris
Cast Komal Amin, Sally Edwards, Yetunde Oduwole
Venue Gielgud Theatre
A co-production with RADA Festival
First Performance 23 June 2016

2016   *My Big Fat Cowpat Wedding* (revival) by Sayan Kent*
Directors Janet Steel & Steve Johnstone
Designer Abigail King
Cast Sukhraj Dhillon, Genevieve Helson, Shri Patel, Graeme Rose
Venues Newhampton Arts Centre, Wolverhampton & thirty-seven village halls & community centres
Co-production with Black Country Touring
First Performance (of revival) 28 September 2016

2017   *Ready or Not* by Naylah Ahmed*
Regret and loss collide with fear and paranoia in a domestic setting, where three characters deal with their personal battles against a backdrop of the war on terror.
Director Helena Bell
Designer Sophia Lovell Smith based on initial ideas by Rajha Shakiry
Lighting Katherine Williams   **Video** Daniel Denton
Sound Chris Drohan
Cast Joan Blackham, Adam Karim, Natasha Rickman
Venues Arcola Theatre, Plymouth Drum & UK tour
First Performance 5 April 2017
Off West End Theatre Award nomination for Best Actress (Joan Blackham)

2017   *Bitched* by Sharon Raizada*
A witty, unflinching look at personal ambition, motherhood and family, asking the question: can women really have it all?
Director Juliet Knight
Designer Naomi Kuyck-Cohen   **Lighting** Jai Morjaria
Sound Rebecca Smith
Cast Shireen Farkhoy, Darren Douglas, Viss Elliot Safavi, Robert Mountford

Venue Tristan Bates Theatre
First Performance 25 October 2017

2018 *Sundowning* by Nessah Muthy*
A compelling play about love, loneliness and guilt between three generations of women dealing with the impact of Alzheimer's disease.
Director Helena Bell
Designer Rajha Shakiry **Video Designer** Daniel Denton
Lighting Pablo Fernandez Baz   **Sound** Dinah Mullen
Movement Yarit Dor.
Cast Hazel Maycock, Nadia Nadif, Aasiya Shah
Venues Tristan Bates Theatre, Plymouth Drum & UK tour
First Performance 10 October 2018
Two Off West End Theatre Award nominations for Best Actress (Hazel Maycock) & Best Sound Design (Dinah Mullen)

2019 *Homing Birds* by Rukhsana Ahmad*
A young refugee returns to Afghanistan in search of identity and belonging.
Director Helena Bell   **Designer** Helen Coyston
Lighting Tanya Joelle Stephenson **Sound** Dinah Mullen
Cast Suzanne Ahmet, Mona Khalili, John O'Mahony, Jay Varsani
Venues Tara Theatre, Plymouth Drum & UK tour
First Performance 9 October 2019
Asian Media Award Nominated for Best Stage Production

2020 **Kali SOLOS Series**
–2021 SOLOS was a series of monologues commissioned from Kali writers as a response to the restrictions imposed by COVID-19, and performed and self-recorded in isolation by regular Kali actors. These short videos were released throughout this year and can be seen on the Kali Theatre website: www.kalitheatre.co.uk

Jakinta by Bettina Gracias
Whilst getting ready for a virtual date, a woman spills cheeky, laugh-out-loud reflections on love, womanhood and sexuality.
Director Helena Bell   **Cast** Sakuntala Ramanee
Premiered 17 April 2020

Walking with Jelly Babies by Sayan Kent
Uncle Madhu, the beloved character from *My Big Fat Cowpat Wedding* returns to talk about that eventful country reception and more importantly . . . his favourite sweet!
Director Helena Bell   **Cast** Aaron Virdee
Premiered 24 April 2020

Last Thursday by Rukhsana Ahmad
Powerful and passionate, tender and funny, *Last Thursday* catches a glimpse into the life of a key worker.
Director Helena Bell   **Cast** Suzanne Ahmet
Premiered 15 May 2020

The Last Clap by Nessah Muthy
Beginning from the last round of applause from theatre audiences to the last Thursday clap for care workers and the NHS, a young woman navigates a transition from centre stage as an actress to the frontline as a care worker. *The Last Clap* was featured in Online @ the SPACE UK's online festival.
Director Helena Bell   **Cast** Mona Goodwin
Premiered 5 June 2020

Dear Joe by Miriam Babooram
Part virtual love letter, part confession, *Dear Joe* offers an entertaining and realistic glimpse into the challenges (and guilty pleasures!) that comes with adjusting to family life in lockdown.
Director Helena Bell   **Cast** Yasmin Wilde
Premiered 26 June 2020

On Hold by Veronica J. Dewan
Deeply moving and sensitive, *On Hold* depicts the brutal reality of living with existing mental health issues in lockdown.
Director Helena Bell   **Cast** Aasiya Shah
Premiered 3 July 2020

The Three Ps by Kiran Benawra
The Three Ps is a student's impassioned speech to her fellow college students which tackles race, politics and contemporary living in Britain.
Director Helena Bell   **Cast** Komal Amin
Premiered 14 July 2020

The Tribe by Sarah Isaac

From a family of doctors working on the frontline, a heartfelt tribute to the sacrifice, dedication and determination of NHS workers whilst focusing on the people behind the profession.
Director Helena Bell   **Cast** Shelley King
Premiered 24 July 2020

Cheek to Cheek by Sharmila Chauhan

Featuring a British South Asian woman as she prepares to join a Black Lives Matter march, this monologue gives an honest and unflinching insight into racial hierarchy, privilege and anti-blackness through the lens of interracial relationships and family ties.
Director Natasha Kathi-Chandra   **Cast** Shalini Peiris
Premiered 30 October 2020

Educating Britain by Alia Bano

Humorous and poignant, *Educating Britain* takes a no holds barred look at the realities of modern-day teaching, its challenges, and its restrictions within a system where teachers are expected to do more than teach.
Director Helena Bell   **Cast** Mariam Haque
Premiered 20 November 2020

Me and Ed by Atiha Sen Gupta

Me and Ed explores the significance of a statue being torn down by Black Lives Matter demonstrators through the eyes of an Indo-Caribbean woman. Skilfully told through childhood memories and adult realisations, the statue becomes more than a physical attribute of the environment, but a reminder of the cultural and racial prejudices experienced by a member of the community it presides over.
Director Helena Bell   **Cast** Komal Amin
Premiered 27 November 2020

Social Distancing by Emteaz Hussain

Combining humour and adolescent honesty, Social Distancing explores the growing pains of childhood friendships and teenage tiffs and how the need to fit in with the cool kids often comes at a price.
Director Helena Bell   **Cast** Ashna Rabheru
Premiered 4 December 2020

* Indicates plays available from the Kali Script Shop on their website

The Monologues

River on Fire

Rukhsana Ahmad

Seema   Fifty. Indian. A writer, intellectual and bohemian. Two marriages. Three children. Glamorous. Has led an exciting and unconventional life.

To Whom   Direct address to theatre audience.

Where   Bombay, India. A hospital bed in the middle of the city.

When   1992 – the Bombay riots.

What Has Just Happened   Seema is seriously ill in hospital. She had recently returned to Bombay for the filming of her epic screenplay – a Bollywood reworking of the Greek myth of Antigone, in which her youngest daughter Kiran, a UK actor, is starring. Kiran and her brother Bobby grew up with their Muslim father's family in the UK. Her eldest daughter Zara was born here in Bombay, married a Hindu and has remained a devout Hindu.

Seema Siddiqui *dies.*

There is a crack of thunder and lightning.

She throws off her shroud and rises from the dead.

Seema   So! It gets closer to the moment of truth. I might even be able to tell you soon who waits across the river: God, or Raam, or Allah, or, just some dumb neutrons and protons, whizzing around in silence!

I must say heaven sounds very nice right now. Bombay's been such a hell-hole since December when they pulled that mosque down at Ayodhya. All the Muslims came out in protest – even the ones who never care to step inside one. It's been dreadful!

Scans the audience. Fans herself elegantly. Switches to a slightly affected voice and manner.

Sometimes I wish I'd been born into a nice, middle-class English family. Life's so much easier in England – especially if you're loaded. They hardly ever fight over religion – not these days. And no one would dream of shouting, 'Death to the traitor!' – like some Muslims do if a fellow believer decides to opt out of the faith.

That really bothers me. Why should your birth determine your faith? Can any of you see the point of that? If I were God I'd rather have my worshippers choose me. 'Pick your moment, I'd say to them – confirmation, bar mitzvah, initiation, bismillah, navjot – however your elders describe it – and choose me yourself or turn away from me, if you will. But don't pray to me simply because your forefathers did that before you!'

At least, that's been the logic of my life.

I was born a Hindu and raised as one. I even married a Hindu and stayed married to him – well, until I went back to university. That politicised me. I became an atheist – and our marriage fell apart. My mother went to every temple, every dargah and every shrine in the whole of Rajasthan, making offerings, tying knots in threads and cutting deals with saints. It got worse. I fell in love with a Muslim, bless him. I married him and became a Buddhist. And I stayed a Buddhist for several years till I came back – in maturity – to my old faith, atheism.

Ooh! That's just a wee bit scary right now! But I've left it too late to worry about it – I reckon. We shall see how it goes.

First presented by Kali Theatre in October 2000 at Lyric Hammersmith, Leicester Haymarket and UK tour.

Another Paradise

Sayan Kent

Abi Tomlinson   Forties, middle class. Warm, caring, natural. Works at the Eden bird sanctuary. Loves all creatures.

To Whom   Lisa Grundy. Twenty-seven. Smart, office type, trendy glasses, hair tied up, calm and detached. She works in customer services.

Where   UK. Leamington Spa. The Alien Registration Office. Cold and impersonal with a luminescent white wall.

When   The near future/present day.

What Has Just Happened   Set in an imaginary and dystopian world where government surveillance is a part of everyday existence and unwanted citizens can, quite literally, be sent to Coventry, the play explores themes of state intervention, freedom of thought, civil liberties and human rights. Access to all areas of a person's life must be approved of by a biometric reader. When Abi's biometric information gets lost in a glitch, she literally loses her identity and is brought to the Alien Registration Office for questioning. Lisa has Abi's file in front of her.

This extract has been adapted to a monologue from the original scene with Lisa.

Abi   Don't think you know me because you know what washing powder I buy, or which TV channels I watch or how many hotels I've stayed in. It's what that file doesn't tell you that counts. You might know how many lovers I've had but you don't know how much I loved them. You might know which brand of chocolate I buy, but you don't know what I taste when I eat it. You don't know my favourite joke, you don't know what cripples me with laughter and you'll never know which photograph I cry over. You think you know my political persuasions but you don't know what burns inside me, what eats me up, what consumes me with passion, what makes me who I am. You . . . will never know me.

She sits.

This is unbelievable. That woman arrested me in my own home.

Explaining slowly and emphatically to **Lisa**.

I am Abigail Tomlin. Entirely. I'm not divided, I'm completely certain. I know who I am. Just scan me back in, I want to rejoin my life. Biometric readers often reject me. I'm one of those people who just doesn't get along with technology. I'm a nature person. I like waves on the beach. Singing dolphins.

Lisa *gives her a blank look.*

Do you do this on purpose?

I'm not going anywhere without my past. Scarred as it is. My . . . school . . . my . . . aunt Jasmine in Broadstairs. My parking offences for God's sake. (*Desperate.*) It's all I've got.

Are you trying to brainwash me? I'll fight it all the way. I. Am. Abi Tomlin.

She sees a bowl of apples on the desk.

Are those apples real? I'm allergic to apples. Abigail Tomlin is allergic to apples.

Give me one, I'll prove I'm Abi Tomlin. But if I die, it'll be your fault.

She picks up an apple and bites.

Music.

She has another bite. She begins to relax and becomes languid, sensuous.

This is delicious. I haven't had an apple in years. Last time I did I was sick as a pig. Thank you.

First presented by Kali Theatre in March 2009 at Manchester Contact, Vanbrugh Theatre and on tour.

Black-i

Sharon Raizada

Naz   Male. Seventeen. British Bengali, Muslim and working class. He lives in Shadwell in London's East End with his mother and sisters. He's scruffy, hassled and needs a shave.

To Whom   Rose. Fifteen. White, comes from a privileged background and lives in a luxury mansion block in London's West End. She wears outsize shades, a silk scarf, long sleeves, long gloves and boots. She has a Gucci bag and a Snoopy toy dog laid out on a picnic rug.

Where   London W1. The empty rooftop of the mansion block where Rose lives.

When   June. A dark night around 4 a.m.

What Has Just Happened   Naz has come to the mansion roof to fix a TV satellite dish. He startles Rose who has snuck up onto the roof to escape the confines of her flat, where her over-protective mother and stepfather insist she stays indoors in daylight. At first she is awkward in his presence; she lies about her age telling him she's eighteen. But when she offers Naz some vodka, and he accepts, they begin to talk freely with Rose telling Naz about her family problems and her actual age of fifteen. Both characters have recently lost their fathers.

This extract has been adapted to a monologue from the original scene with Rose.

Naz   When I was fifteen   yeah . . . Fifteen –

I had the best fucking night of my life on vodka –

I'm on the roof at this party. With this girl and she's peng you get me –

And I'm so wasted I can't even see. And there's scaffolding all over the roof and down the front . . . Not a roof like this – s'a normal house . . . doing a loft or something.

All my bredrin are on weed downstairs and we got a bottle of Smirnoff, doing shots –

And I don't know what the fuck's going on but next thing I know I'm climbing over it . . . and over the edge. And it's all sky and stars and metal bars –

And she's shouting shit but I don't hear a thing.

It's mad!

It's like being in space . . . and I fucking hate heights. And next thing I know I'm on the ground -

. . . S' the best fucking feeling.

If I had a time machine –

I'd go back to that party and break it. Just break the machine. Stay there, forever.

Getting fucked.

Ain't nothing better –

. . . Party. Bredrin. Fifteen –

Dat's it.

Enjoy it yeah. Cos gets shit from here.

. . . I don't see no one no more.

Dad passed. And I'm man of the house.

. . . I'm sick of this shit.

Ain't no laughs no more . . .

Shouldn't drink, it makes me depressed –

Don't see no one innit! No parties now. Rash and Jas and Kobi. Kaled, Javed, Mo.

Some of them got kids and shit, s'different now.

Looks around for his stuff.

Gotta go.

Ain't no tubes for an hour.

You ain't met my mum . . . I ain't back when she's up, my ears gonna bleed –

Heads for door.

Problems! Wanna know bout fucking *problems*?

I work my ass off day and night to pay for a *fucking fridge* . . .

A'ight –

(*At door.*) I can get one for 50 quid. But no, this slick woman come round. I'll help you out, she says, we're all part of the community. So Mum gets a new one from Curry's innit.

Cash on the door. No contract, paperwork, no fucking APR!

(*Takes one step.*) School uniforms . . . same again –

My sisters look good . . . she don't say a word. I don't see, cos I ain't ever in!

Probably four or five times she did it –

And ain't the woman comes back. S'motherfuckers with baseball bats. You don't pay – they break your legs. Or Mum's legs.

Sister's.

And Monday morning 8 a.m. – I pay and fucking pay FOR HER –

s' three hours you get me –

Paid five times over – and it don't go down. And I still gotta pay and it still ain't enough –

So *fuck* your bling life and your *bling fucking bullshit*.

First presented by Kali Theatre in October 2010 at Ovalhouse.

Speed

Iman Qureshi

Sarah Twenties. British South Asian. A publicist for MTV. She looks dazzling and elegant in a cocktail dress and high heels.

To Whom Direct address to theatre audience.

Where London, Shoreditch. The basement of a bar being used for speed dating: 'Tonight: South Asian Speed Dating'.

When Early December. A Thursday evening around 7.30 p.m. It's cold and dark outside.

What Has Just Happened Sarah was ditched a week ago, after a six-month affair with a married TV producer. She has come to this speed-dating session to lick her wounds. She is in the mood to drink and during the first half of the scene she systematically downs a line of clear shots she has pre-ordered at the bar.

Sarah You know I don't think I've ever been loved. Fucked, yes, loads. In abundance. Lucky me. But loved?

Shrugs, then remembers last weekend.

That old TV producer. Skin like a rotting plum – like it was slipping and sliding all over his bones. With these coarse wiry grey hairs sprouting out of his chest. (*Grimaces.*)

He can promise you the world when he wants you – and you believe him. Because he owns the world. And you're just programmed to want to be up on top with him. No one ever tells you that all you'll ever be good for is sitting on top of him with your clothes off.

Beat.

And he chases you and makes you feel special for a while.

And eventually, he gets what he wants. And then he just owns you along with the rest of the world. Pops you up on the shelf like another trophy. And there you sit, getting all dusty. Hoping that one day he'll notice you again, take you down. Look at you like he once used to. Want you like he once used to.

Beat.

Last weekend feels like such a blur. I was asking him about his wife. His famous news presenter wife. I was asking him about how he fell in love with her; why he fell in love with her. And he was saying well, everything – her voice, her smell, her soft white skin. And in the hospital, when she gave birth to his baby boy. Her hair was tied up in this messy girly ponytail. And her cheeks were flushed pink. And her forehead glistened with sweat. And he remembered thinking that he had never felt this much love in his life; he felt like it was bursting out of his chest. And there I was wrenching the details from him, torturing myself, wanting to know more and more. Wanting to know how, if he really loved her, he could bear to fuck someone thirty years younger than him, while his beautiful chiselled perfect wife was sitting, waiting for him to come home. But really, really wanting to know whether he could ever love me like he loved her. And what it was about her that made him fall in love. So maybe I could try and be that for him. Be her. Or something like her. Because that love – the love he was talking about. I've never felt it. Never has anyone loved me like that.

Beat.

And I remember he was telling me this – how he loved her –while standing on the sidewalk outside the bar on Park Lane.

Traffic was shooting by – buses, trucks. And I was shouting questions over the noise. Or maybe I was shouting with anger. Or fear, I don't know. And I felt sick. Like nauseous. Or out of breath. You know that feeling when you're up on a mountain? And however much you breathe, however deep you breathe, it's like it's not enough. And he was telling me that he still loves her but he's not in love with her – and I can't really see much difference – and all of a sudden I just couldn't take it anymore. And I put my hand over my mouth, but it was too late, and the next thing I know, I was kneeling over the curb being sick in the road.

What a sight. There I was, six-inch heels, six vodkas down, six cucumber makis back up. Six months. Six months of this. Six months of his lies. And still, I looked up at him to say 'I'm sorry'. But he was looking down at me with this face. Not pity. Not disgust. Not anger. But like a face that said, 'This isn't worth it'. And he said, 'I'll call you tomorrow'. And he never.

And he just left me there, with my face against the cool concrete of the ground.

And the curb was so comforting in that moment. Like I could rest my head against it and it would look after me. Or like I could take his head and smash it against the concrete. And then hers too. Take her by the hair and smash – there go her pretty white teeth. Smash. Her jaw. Smash, her skull, her brain, her eyes – everything he loved about her – smash. Both of them. Smash. Kicked to the curb, nothing quite like it.

Beat.

But that was me, wasn't it? Literally, literally lying by the curb.

Smelling of cucumber-scented bile, feeling like my chest had been smashed in, and aching, aching, everywhere.

First presented by Kali Theatre in February 2013 at Tristan Bates Theatre.

Nazma

Nessah Muthy

Nazma   Thirty-three. British Asian. Learning difficulties. Married to Bilal.

To Whom   Her Mother. Nazma is leaving a voice message.

Where   London. A women's refuge.

When   Present day.

What Has Just Happened   Nazma has been taken from the house she shares with Bilal to a refuge.

This piece was originally commissioned for *Twelve*, a series of monologues about honour killings in the UK.

Voiceover   Welcome to the mailbox. The person you have called cannot accept your call. Please leave your message after the beep.

Nazma   Mama?

Beep.

She sighs. She redials.

Voiceover   Welcome to the –

Nazma   Mama –

She sighs. She redials.

Voiceover   Welcome to the mailbox. The person you're calling is unable to take your call. Please leave your message after the beep. To re-record your message, key hash at any time.

Beep.

Nazma   Mama? Mama? Mama are you ok? Mama where have you gone? Mama? My hair is knotty. It's so knotty, I cannot get the knots out and the ladies cannot get the knots out either. Mama, I don't want to get in trouble for having knotty hair. Bilal got some of the knots out, but that was ages ago and new knots have grown, so many knots. I don't think he liked to get the knots, he did it, he did it, quite, argh, argh. (*She scrapes* *her fingers through her hair*.) Even though I showed him, I showed him the right way, but he still, still, argh, argh. (*She scrapes her fingers through her hair*.) 'Retard.' Retard is not my name silly. 'Retard.'

Beat.

There are lots of ladies here that cry, they just cry, Mama, some of them have babies and they cry.

She cries like a baby.

I cannot really sleep because of all the cries.

Beat.

I don't like the bed. The bed is small. The bed is smelly. The bed is farty, like bad Papa farts. Where is Papa? I love Papa. I like the bed at home with you. I do also like the bed with Bilal too; the bed was big with Bilal. He holds me and sometimes rubs me. I like the rubbing. I like the nice rubbing. Not the rough rubbing. I try to tell him, I try, the poopie comes out there and he chases me, chase, chase. He has a long poo poo, Mama, a poo poo that's stuck to him, where a front bottom should be.

She giggles.

Bilal is, I think, I think, a bad boy, Mama, a naughty boy. A wicked boy. Bilal is very punished. Bilal is very tricked.

Beat.

He likes to: 'Fuck boys!' 'Fuck boys!'

Beat.

I think I love Bilal. I think I do. Bilal is a soldier, Bilal is a sailor, Bilal is a prince. A prince, Mama.

Beat.

I'd like to kiss Bilal . . .

Beat.

I don't like his Rolex. His Rolex is naughty. If I be naughty, the Rolex is very naughty. Sometimes I don't mean to be naughty. There was blood, Mama, blood all in the toilet and the Rolex got me on my chin. It's a very bad Rolex. Mama. Oh Mama, I love you!

Beat.

I tried to tell Bilal on Tuesdays, Wednesdays and Fridays I go to the centre and that Mina will be so cross. But Bilal said no more centre.

Beat.

I still wear the shiny ring. It's so shiny. But Bilal doesn't always wear his shiny ring. Bilal has a friend from Tesco's, his name is Will. They shut the bedroom door. And they say: 'Fuck off' It's not very nice. 'Fuck off, fatty retard, or I'll stab you in the heart!' I hope the Rolex will get them . . .

Beat.

I just rub myself and eat the twiglets because there isn't any dinner . . . 'Who is that?' I heard Will say. Bilal says, 'That is my sister' I am not the sister though am I, Mama? I am the bride? I am the princess aren't I, Mama? On the phone I said the prayer and I wore the lipstick and the jewels and the silk and the happiness, the smiles, the smiley on your face . . . the smiley on Papa's face . . .

Beat.

I'm not allowed to answer the door. I'm not allowed to answer the phone. That's just the rules . . . But then, one day, the door is: BANG! BANG! BANG!

BANG! BANG! BANG! I peep through the curtain and it is Mina and another lady and they wave. And she's got Minstrels. I have to open the door. I have to get those Minstrels. She says her and the lady are happy to have found me. She says they haven't got much time and they ask me all these questions, Mama. The lady has a pen, scribble, scribble, scribble and a recorder. I really want to touch the buttons on the recorder, but I am not allowed to touch the buttons. Some are easy-peasy questions, so easy: What is your name? Nazma Mahmud. How old are you, Nazma Mahmud? Thirty-three.

Beat.

The next questions are strange questions, Mama. I do not know these questions:

'What is a husband?' I don't know

She giggles.

I like to watch the lines go up on the recorder. I speak LOUD! And I speak . . . slow . . . Bilal is a husband? 'What is a marriage?'

She giggles.

She shrugs.

Then she asks a rudey question, a really, really rudey question . . .

She giggles.

The poopie bottom is for the poopie and the front bottom is for the pee pee.

She giggles.

The lady turns the recorder off and I cannot see the lines anymore. Mina gets a bag, I say that's Bilal's bag, but she says it doesn't matter. Quick, quick, she puts my knickers and my vest and my asthma pump in. Just for a little while, just a little trip. So now I am here, I am here with the babies and the ladies and the crying . . .

Voiceover   The mailbox is now full and cannot accept any more messages at this time. Goodbye.

Nazma   Mama . . . Mama . . . my hair is very knotty . . . Mama . . .

Distant sound of babies crying.

She cries.

Mama . . .

First presented by Kali Theatre in April 2015 at Brentford Watermans, Birmingham mac and Rich Mix.

The Survivor

Anu Kumar Lazarus

Bal Forties. British Asian. From the North East of England. A survivor of honour-based violence.

To Whom Women who have been subjected to similar experiences.

Where A community centre or local theatre.

When Present day. Early evening.

What Has Just Happened Bal has been invited to share her experiences of domestic violence and give advice on how to leave.

NB: This piece was originally commissioned for *Twelve* (a series of monologues about honour killings in the UK). This account was inspired by a survivor. The writer interviewed Bal using a verbatim theatre technique to capture and preserve her authentic voice. Bal's journey continues. More information can be found at www.bkhtraining.co.uk.

Bal I'm a survivor of honour-based violence.

I come from the North East. . . . me and my sister, we are still in danger. I'm married now and we are really happy. I . . . I'd like to help other people that are in the same position as I was.

I was married off to someone, aged seventeen, I think he was twenty-six or so . . . He was from India, so he got a British passport by marrying me.

I was taken out of school from when I was thirteen, so I didn't really know anything else apart from what went on in my house and family.

I think the thing that saved me really was the irony of the fact that I was allowed to work . . . (so that immigration could see my wage slips and they knew that he would be supported) and that I could drive. I had to drive, it was my job to get everyone to the gurdwara and back and do all the jobs, like the family shopping, which meant I needed a car.

If I meet girls about to go through with forced marriages, I ask them: Do they understand what they will have to go through?

A man they don't know will be touching her, whenever and wherever he wants.

He will basically own her and he might think it would be ok to be violent towards her . . .

I just couldn't have stayed. Eight and a half years of horrific abuse . . . What I did took three months of planning . . .

I looked for a job in London and I went there and had an interview and I got the job. I looked in *Loot* magazine – do they still have that now? I found a flat and slowly gathered everything in the house with my name on it. I didn't want to be traceable.

Then I left, I went to the police and told them that I would get reported as a missing person, but that I wasn't.

I was leaving to be safe.

And that was it . . . no one ever found me.

Being found terrified me – I once saw some brothers going off to find their younger sister that had run away: they took a car full of swords and baseball bats. Swords and baseball bats . . . can you believe it? Brutal, like monsters.

You have to remember, the average age of the perpetrators is twenty-two . . . It's kids . . . brothers . . . cousins . . . swords and baseball bats . . .

I left my sister, that was hard, because she has learning difficulties, but I told social services and they still look after her. Social services told me that my family had moved away from the house where we lived because of the shame. The shame of being parents of a girl who had escaped to freedom . . .

If ever I meet a girl now that has managed to escape, or is trying to, I say, do you know where your passport and papers are and how to access any money? And can you be alone?

Can you be completely alone so that no one can find you, because that's what you need to do . . . and the being alone goes on for a long, long time. Until one day, someone breaks in to your personal world and you feel you can trust them.

Overall, though, I would say, the things I miss most are the culture, the language. They are brilliant things . . . and my mum. I kept thinking why didn't she protect me? . . . but I think she was very unhappy in her marriage and she was married at twelve in her village.

I did it all by myself . . . so it can be done.

First presented by Kali Theatre in April 2015 at Brentford Watermans, Birmingham mac and Rich Mix.

The Girl

Sonali Bhattacharyya

The Girl Twenty-two but looks younger. British Asian. Londoner.

To Whom Female refuge worker.

Where London. A women's refuge.

When Present day.

What Has Just Happened The Girl has entered the office of the refuge, angry and on the defensive.

This piece was originally commissioned for *Twelve*, a series of monologues about honour killings in the UK.

Girl Don't give a shit what she said, dirty sket. She's a whore and she's a liar. Got it in for me, man. Ain't it obvious?

Why? Truth hurts, innit? Believes that guy's gonna whisk her away and marry her. Fallen for that big heart, big dick routine, big time. He's gonna use her just like every other guy in her life, stupid bitch. Thinks she's special 'cos she's 'in love'? Jokes, man. They're all the same – sooner she works that out, the better. Doing her a favour, she just don't know it yet. Better face up now before she gets her hopes up and shit. Ask anyone. I was minding my own, trying to make a call, and she just went for me.

Beat.

What is this anyway? Positive discrimination for stupid lying bitches? Should be looking into why she's going round making accusations. Who knows what sneaky shit she's up to? Whatevs, man. Soon as I get myself together I'll be out of your hair. Nothing like that dreamy-faced cow. I get the big picture, yeah? I know what it's all about.

Long beat.

What's that? Iced tea? (*Beat.*) That for me? (*Hesitates.*)

Yeah, I'm thirsty, man. Want to turn the heating down in this place – waste of taxpayers' money.

She accepts the iced tea.

How'd you know I like iced tea?

Beat.

She takes a long swig. Starts to soften.

Just . . . having a shitty day, y'know? No one's business but my own. Wanted five minutes to talk to someone like-minded, and like hell that's anyone round here. Always got some bitch listening to their music, or doing their nails on the fucking stairs. Feel like my head's gonna explode sometimes. Like I got nowhere to go but . . . boom. Exact time she has to wander over, innit?

Beat.

It's my birthday. Shut up, not telling you.

Beat.

Alright, I'm twenty-two. That's why all these stupid kids get on my nerves, yeah? And the others . . . Old enough to be my mum and still taking shit? Sorry, yeah, but I ain't got much sympathy. Time comes when you gotta stop acting the victim, right? (*Beat.*)

Don't do birthdays, anyway. Firingi bullshit, man. Decadent rubbish. Only person ever bought me a birthday present was . . . him. Yeah. Faruk. Sentimental twat. (*Beat.*) Jewellery and stuff. Y'know, things I could hide.

Beat.

Nah, wasn't him I was calling. It's over, man. What's the point in picking that wound? Ending it was my choice. You lot can think what you like. Got my own mind. That's a problem for you, yeah? Want us all to be nice little Malalas, making you feel good about yourselves and shit. Don't get me wrong, it's not like I'm ungrateful or nothing. Just don't want to end up some woolly-assed, croc-wearing cow, you get me? Hardest thing in here's keeping a sense of your own identity. Might've had to change my name, but my DNA's still the same. And half of it's Dad's, yeah? What am I supposed to do? Pretend I'm someone I'm not?

Beat.

Got no right, man. You don't know him. All you know is what they put in the police reports – that don't tell you everything about a person. He was an engineer back home. All he gets here is hassle from the Five-Os.

Doesn't need his own flesh and blood sticking the knife in, does he? Better a good wife than some hard-nosed firingi career bitch, anyway. Better a good mum than some alky cow hoping she'll meet Mr Right one day. Yeah, he can be a bully, and he never knows when to back down, but you know what? Sometimes he's got a point.

Beat.

You can hate someone's guts and still respect them . . . Right?

He never asked me to ring, my sis did, 'kay? He just wanted to speak to me, that's all. Stupid cow should stick to her magazines and stop butting her nose in. What's she doing listening in on my private convos, eh? She's the one should be getting a bollocking. I mean. Get. A. Life. Jeez. Sket.

Beat.

Didn't lie. No I didn't.

Beat.

Only 'cos I wanted to hear him out first. That so wrong? Didn't tell him jack shit. Don't care what the bitch says. He don't know nothing about this place. I know your confidentiality risk assessment crap back to back, man. Signed your fucking agreement, didn't I? Think I'm stupid or something? I get it, yeah? Big bad wolf's out there and he wants in on the little piggies. But if that happens it won't be 'cos of me.

Beat.

He's changed, man. He's sorry. Never meant to hurt me, things just got out of hand. Even said 'happy birthday'. Know what that takes for a guy like him? Never heard him admit he's wrong, my whole life. He just wants to be able to talk eye to eye, yeah? I'm as bad as him if I say no, aren't I? Gotta meet him halfway. That so wrong? He's still my dad.

Beat.

Why'd I lie, man? (*Beat.*) You all made your minds up about me, I get that, I ain't stupid. But I ain't scared of you. Can't threaten me, I got options. You think you got me cornered, but I already worked out my next move.

Beat.

You got a guy? Made a home with him? Kids? (*Beat.*) Nah. You don't have to say. I can tell. Nice. Must feel good, looking up at that clock, seeing it's five thirty-five? Another half an hour and you're out of this shit-hole. Don't lie, know what you're thinking. Feeling sorry for the poor bitches like me, left here, nowhere to go. It's this or . . . what? (*Melodramatic voice.*) Home with that monster. Hell on earth.

Beat.

We had good times, yeah? Mum making pakore in the kitchen, Sun TV on, my sisters playing carom, Dad snoring on the sofa. Sometimes he woke up happy. Sober. Sometimes he'd give me a fiver and send me out for chips. Even when he didn't . . . (*Beat.*) Whatever went down, we were a family. Still are. Maybe we just belong together, whatever happens. That's what duty means, right? You try to make out we got all these choices, but that's bullshit, man. That's just what lucky people tell themselves so they feel clever. You don't get to choose this shit. You're born into it. (*Beat.*) Nah. That's not right either. You got one choice. Accept it, or run. And I'm tired of running, yeah?

First presented by Kali Theatre in April 2015 at Brentford Watermans, Birmingham mac and Rich Mix.

The Dishonoured

Aamina Ahmad

Gulzar Twenty-two. Pakistani. She is wearing a kameez but no shalwar. Frightened, imprisoned and alone.

To Whom Her male captors – Colonel Tariq (thirty-eight) and Captain Badhshah Gul (twenty-nine) both of whom are officers in the Pakistan Intelligence Agency (ISI).

Where Pakistan, Lahore. A prison cell.

When 2009. Night.

What Has Just Happened Gulzar's sister, Shaida (a prostitute in the wrong place at the wrong time), has been murdered by a CIA operative. Gulzar, the only witness to the CIA agent's presence at the scene of the crime, has been imprisoned by the ISI, and later abused by her guards. When Colonel Tariq and his lackey arrive claiming they will free her, she sees right through their ploy.

This extract has been adapted into a monologue from an original scene with Gulzar's captors.

Gulzar I didn't think I would see you again . . . I thought you'd forgotten me. No one ever came to take me out of the police station. I was at Central all this time. Till today. Their cells are crowded . . . this is nice. My own room. A bed.

When can I leave?

So never.

You're going to kill me.

Did you find out? What happened? To my sister? Why she was killed? What about the investigation? There wasn't one. Because the American was someone important. Because Shaida wasn't.

If you wanted, you could ask me about my sister. I could tell you about her.

I keep trying to see her. But I can't remember anything . . . except for the way I found her. I want to forget that but I can't. I hear her voice though. Sometimes. When I close my eyes. I hear her reading her poetry; she used to get very serious, speak very slow when she read her work. I don't know if it was very good, I don't know about things like that, saab, but she read it like it was. Like it was very important, like she was really someone, saab.

Bit of a show-off, I suppose. But even I had to admit that when she spoke like that . . . in her shaeri's voice . . . she seemed really . . . beautiful. Her heart was so – hidden all the time, but then all of a sudden she was there, reading these words . . . giving it to you.

Gulzar *lunges for* **Captain Badhshah Gul** *but he moves out of the way and* **Tariq** *intervenes. She starts to ineffectively strike* **Tariq** *as she curses. He doesn't defend himself but lets her strike and push him around the room.*

Gulzar *Haram zadeh, behencahud, gashti, dalleh, behenchaud, behenchaud, behenchaud . . .*

She runs out of steam, she's breathless, exhausted.

Come on, come on, saab, come on, captain, you too. Come on. I'm here. Look at me. You've made me a whore like Shaida now. Look, look. You'd still have me, saab, wouldn't you. Marry me to your son. You'd still have me for your daughter

Home.

Oh thank you, saab. Thank you. That's very decent of you. It's all I've been thinking about. Home. And my mother. My Amma. All day, all these hours alone, I think about her. I wonder what she's doing right now at this minute. Cutting okra, milking the goat. Praying. Crying. I feel like I'm trying to reach her. And I keep thinking she'll feel me, hear me if I can just think about her hard enough. Because I can't stop worrying about her. My poor Amma. I think about how I wasn't there to tell her about Shaida, to hold her through it, that maybe she's been crying for me. That she must look around the walls of our tiny house and feel terrified. That this is a home from which children vanish into thin air. She must ache from it. And I know she's praying because that's all she knows to do. Because people like us have no one but God. And I know what she'll say if she sees me coming up the street. God is great, God is great. And she'll cry tears of happiness. He brought you back to me. Miracles happen. And it's true, saab, not about miracles because I don't know much about things like that but it's true that my Amma's waiting for me, praying for me, that she's remembering my face with her hands, that she's saying my name again and again, calling to me because there are people who love me, even me, someone like me . . . and who will never forget me.

First presented by Kali Theatre in March 2016 at Leicester Curve, Arcola Theatre and on tour.

Ready or Not

Naylah Ahmed

Yusuf Male. Early twenties. British Asian. Muslim. Small, skinny frame, dressed in white Arab-style tunic, over cropped trousers, socks, trainers and a prayer cap. He is sitting tied to a chair. Feet and hands bound.

To Whom Pat. Female. Sixties. White. Divorced. Ex teacher. Physically strong. She has been drawn into the murky world of online, right-wing extremist chat rooms since the death of her only son Jack. Pat wears trousers, a plain blouse and a man's cardigan down to her knees.

Where UK. Pat's living room in a small suburban house. There is a door leading to the small hallway, and rest of the house. There is a framed photo of Jack smiling. On the desk are piles of cuttings from newspapers, and a landline telephone. In a corner of the room is a mound of bouquets, all whites and yellows accompanied by a mini-landslide of unopened cards.

When 2016. Late morning. A bright day.

What Has Just Happened Yusuf has been calling at houses asking people to sign a petition against the British government's use of drones in Afghanistan and Pakistan. When he calls at Pat's house he becomes a victim of her crazed grief and prejudice. It's the morning of her dead son's memorial. Jack was a soldier who died in Afghanistan from an unexploded mine. Pat has never had his body returned and in a moment of madness she overpowers Yusuf and takes him hostage. She is unpredictable and violent, pouring soup over Yusuf's head and almost drowning him in a bucket of water. Between these episodes she calms and removes his gag, talking with him more rationally. Yusuf has tried to appease, pleading with her to release him but to no avail. Here he decides to change tack.

This extract has been adapted into a monologue from an original scene with Pat.

Yusuf I can't believe you used to teach – or maybe I can.

I knew teachers like you. Do everything by the book but there's just something in their tone that tells you – even as a kid – they don't like you.

Please tell me you didn't have any 'ethnically' diverse kids? . . . Man, how was that for you? Actually, I bet you enjoyed it – I wonder how many souls you crushed . . . How many names you mispronounced all year.

I went to collect my nephew from junior school this once. His teacher – nice woman by all accounts – she starts calling him Kumar. So I tell her, really politely, miss, it's actually Qamar, not Kumar. So she turns to my nephew and – really loud – she says, 'Kumar, how do you say your name?' My nephew just stares at his feet. So she tells me I'm wrong – she actually tells me to my face that I'm wrong, because she's called him Kumar all year and he hasn't corrected her.

So I point out – on his book bag – that there isn't a 'u' in it, miss. Q A M A R – no Ku for Kumar. Kay-mar would have been an attempt. But Kumar, that's just lazy.

The mispronunciation isn't even what bothered me, Pat. It's how she dealt with being corrected. Anyway, I'm glad you're out of it now, teaching.

There's no need to get upset, Pat. I mean, it's not like I'm talking about you, is it?

It's unpleasant for you, isn't it, that someone – like me – might know something you don't.

Yeah . . . It's just a name, right? A name you're called a thousand times a day in class. A name all the other kids'll call you. Except it's not your name, is it. But you get used to it anyway. And other kids – kids who know better – they start calling you it too. So you learn not to make a fuss – at that young age – not to speak out because miss doesn't like it when she's wrong. Even if she is wrong, Pat. That's not a teacher.

Mrs Wilson never got my name right. I had her for the last two years of primary. She was alright, Mrs Wilson. Man, she was really bad at names though, bless her, and my class was almost totally Asian! But she didn't ever mind being corrected. She wasn't threatened by it. I always knew she was trying.

What made you leave teaching? . . . Did you do something? . . . What did you do, Pat?

Something to a kid?

First presented by Kali Theatre in April 2017 at Plymouth Drum, Arcola Theatre and on tour.

On Hold

Veronica J. Dewan

A Kali SOLOs commission, originally intended for online audiences.

Padma   Early twenties. British Asian. Without family or friends.
Recently admitted to a psychiatric unit following a suicide attempt.

To Whom   Ashley. A nurse in Padma's psychiatric unit. Has a
daughter.

Where   London. A flat.

When   Present day.

What Has Just Happened   Padma has been discharged early from a
psychiatric unit in London following a fire on the ward. Alone and with
no job or family to fall back on, she has no money and is trying to get
connected to the Department for Work and Pensions. When she can't get
through she calls up her former nurse Ashley who has given Padma her
mobile number. The following are a series of FaceTime calls Padma
makes to Ashley over four days.

1.

Padma   Ashley. Where you been? It's nine hours since I got discharged.
I don't know how they get away with it. They said they were making
plans to find me another place to stay. They got my hopes up, Ashley. It's
not ok, is it? Discharged from the psych unit back to the flat I don't feel
safe in. I still got bills to pay and my fucking benefits got stopped
because I was in the hospital and I'm on hold to the DWP and I . . .

Is that an orange? How many oranges have you had today? The one you
gave me was lovely. I needed some vitamin C. What was I saying? Yeah,
I was the one to get kicked out. I know you can't talk about it, it's
confidential. I don't know how you stand it, working in that stinking
place, patients calling you the N-word.

Well, I've been cleaning, keeping the phone on speaker. Why do they
take so long? Can we FaceTime again tomorrow? Ashley?

2.

Padma Hey you! Seventeen hours and forty minutes and no one broken the door down. First time it's been quiet here. Oh, the best news is I found a Christmas pudding, at the back of the cupboard. For eight people. I hate Christmas. I could be dead by then. It's a joke. I'm not gonna do anything now I have my freedom. It says on the label you have to cook Christmas pudding. I don't see why when it's all fruits and nuts. If only I had another orange. Ah, I could do with some brandy butter. Back at the hostel I wasn't allowed brandy butter, it was that mad! I like clotted cream best, it's thick, pale gold, it's what you get in Devon. Devon was the last foster family. They were proper posh. The kids called me a 'filthy little Paki' without even raising their voices. I've taken my meds. Honest. Not the ones I was on before, they were the worst, made me hallucinate. That's why you didn't believe me when it all kicked off. I haven't seen anyone, apart from the social worker. He didn't get it either. I left the flat a mess. But it's not a mess, it's tidy. Marjorie, the one who lives upstairs, I ought to thank her. But I don't wanna disturb her. I like the quiet. What time's your shift finish? Is the alarm going off? Someone trying to escape? Ashley? Oh, ok, you've gone.

3.

Padma Sorry. I'm sorry. I didn't mean to wake you. You said we could FaceTime whenever I was down. I'm feeling down, so fucking down. Marjorie's gone. I looked through the letterbox, place is cleared out. I never thanked her, Ashley. She was lovely, I mean, really caring. That last time, she comes in, sees the state of the place, says I'll be ok, helping me up . . . helping me up off the floor, wrapping me in a blanket . . . she's really gentle leading me to the ambulance.

It's thirty-seven hours and four minutes since I've been home. No. No you can't go. Didn't you hear what I said about Marjorie? I know you're not my mother. I never asked you to be my mother. You'd be a useless fucking mother.

4.

Padma I'm sorry she's ill. I didn't know. Do you play Scrabble with her? I miss us playing Scrabble. The concentration it takes to find a word. D'you remember when Ken smashed his fist down on the board and the pieces flew right off onto the floor. I would have won. I would have won.

5.

Padma   I promise this is the last time. I – I never thanked you for all that with the beds, the fire, me screaming and you grabbing me, telling me it was ok, it was all in my head. It gave you a fright when the firemen burst in all helmets and hoses, you must have been like, is it me, Ashley, am I the one hallucinating now? You apologised, I know, thanks. And you sat up all night with me, held my hand, reciting poems by Lemn? Lemn Sissay. He was an abandoned child, you said.

So. Why? Why did my psychiatrist chuck me out and not her who set fire to my bed ninety-two hours ago? I'm sorry I'll – I'll stop now. Your – your daughter needs you. Oh, did I, did I tell you about the Christmas pudding I found at the back of the cupboard? I've eaten half of it. I'll keep trying the DWP. Padma is on hold.

She hears a sound outside. She opens her front door. She comes back with a box. She opens it. Inside are oranges which she removes one by one. She removes a greeting card from the box. Five twenty-pound notes fall out.

First presented online by Kali Theatre in July 2020.

Dear Joe

Miriam Babooram

A Kali SOLOS commission, originally intended for online audiences.

Anita   Forties, working class. Married to Bill, they have two children. She works in a bar.

To Whom   Joe Wicks MBE. TV fitness instructor. Wicks rose to prominence during the Spring 2020 lockdown when he taught a nation how to exercise from home.

Where   Anita's house.

When   2020. Morning.

What Has Just Happened   Anita has just finished her morning exercise routine with Joe.

Anita   I just, I just love waking up with you. The way you smile at me every morning with that glint of mischief in your eyes. And your hair is all messy like a lion's mane, I just want to run my hands through it. You make me happy Joe. You make me want to be a better person. With you I feel like I can be the best version of myself. You make me feel like I could conquer the world, that rush of adrenalin I get when I'm with you. I love it when we dress up, Joe. It's like you read my mind. Things get so hot and steamy when we're in those costumes. When you were Spiderman and I was Wonder Woman that was really hot, I'd love to get caught up in your web. I did worry that time you dressed up as Scooby Doo though Joe and you started farting all over the room, that was a bit weird to be honest, but I stuck with it because, well, you have to try new things once in a while. And I trust you, Joe, I trust you to take me on this journey. Honestly, Joe, some days when I've been with you I just can't walk after. Those are the best days, when we've had a really good session. Sometimes I just have to scream to get through them. You looked hot in your suit the other day, Joe. And when you took your jacket off the sweat had made your shirt see-through. I can just imagine what your sweat smells like, all manly. I took a screenshot of you like that when you weren't looking. I've got pictures of you all over my bedroom wall, my husband's not too impressed, but what's he going to do? They're all black and white because I printed them off the computer and I don't have any coloured ink, and although you're a bit blurry, Joe, I still know your eyes are smiling at me. And I kiss your picture goodnight.

The other day when we were working out with your whole family, to be honest I did get a bit jealous, but a bit of me wished I had a family like that. My husband, he doesn't join in the workouts, Joe. He just laughs and calls me lard arse, and I laugh too, but it's not funny is it really? I mean, he's no oil painting. He was alright looking when we were younger and he was fun. But he's bald now and he's got a beer belly. Not properly bald, Joe – that would be OK. But bald like he won't admit that he's losing his hair, so he's bald on top and got hair at the sides, a bit like the guy in that Hamlet advert? Do you remember that advert, Joe? It was a classic. He was in a photo booth and he couldn't get his picture taken properly and he ended up having a smoke. I bet you've never smoked have you? I see the way you behave with your kids, Joe, and you just love them. I wish I felt like that. I mean I do love them of course, they're my kids, but I don't really enjoy them, you know. They're teenagers, I think that makes a difference, Joe. They chat back to you. They think you know nothing about the world, like I've experienced nothing in my forty-something years on the planet and they know everything. I can't help thinking, Joe, that if you were my kids' dad and not old baldy face that we'd have a very different life, that they'd be fun kids, that we'd go for walks and laugh all the time. I can't remember the last time I laughed, Joe. Isn't that sad? I mean you bring me joy, you really do, and I love it when we do the Silly Billy, I bring out my best dance moves then. But properly laugh with tears streaming down my face and almost peeing myself. I've just not got much to laugh about. I reckon the bailiffs are going to come any day, Joe. I don't know what we're going to do.

We went on holiday last year, Joe. It was a holiday of a lifetime, we went to Majorca and Bill, that's Mr Baldy, well, he'd just lost his job and we thought he needed cheering up so we got one of those loans you know the ones you see on the telly, where they don't do a credit check. And, well, we didn't realise how much we'd have to pay back. And Baldy Bill still hasn't got any work and I was working down the pub but that's all stopped. I go to the food banks now, Joe. Who would have thought it. That's not the life you dream for yourself is it? But what doesn't kill you makes you stronger or something like that. And I feel stronger, Joe.

Thanks to your workouts. I feel like I can conquer the world. In that half hour, between 9 and 9.30, anything is possible. I'm not a massive fan of those kangaroo jumps, mind, I usually end up holding onto my boobs. I've not got a sports bra, Joe, it's not something I thought about before this thing. But I love you, Joe, you mean so much to me. You're changing my life truly. I just wanted you to know.

First presented online by Kali Theatre in June 2020.

Cheek to Cheek

Sharmila Chauhan

A Kali SOLOS commission, originally intended for online audiences.

Parul Early forties. British Asian. Married to James who is black. They have two children. Parul is dressed in black. She's kind of posh but slips into a more Estuary and Desi accent at times.

To Whom Sand (Sandhya) Parul's sister who had agreed to attend a Black Lives Matter march with her. They are speaking over a video link (FaceTime or equivalent).

Where London. A really nice kitchen. A family space, toys, clothes everywhere, but it's also a space with organic teas, Himalayan salt, etc. We may also see religious images mixed in now and then.

When 2020. Summer. Early afternoon. In the middle of lockdown, just after the murder of George Floyd. BLM marches are everywhere.

What Has Just Happened Parul has prepared a picnic lunch for them both and has just called Sand. She points her phone down onto the kitchen table where a pile of sandwiches lie, packed with a bottle of water and a phone battery.

Parul Shall I pack the dokra or you think sandwiches are enough? I've got some sourdough, with cheese and that sticky pickle you like . . .

These? (*Pointing to some sandwiches in foil.*) They're batata nu shaak – sandwiches.

I know, right?

Not as good as Mum's but . . . Can't always be the 'best', right?

How are they? Mum and Dad? They ok?

They don't say much on the phone. I wish I could see them, but maybe it's easier for them this way.

Beat.

. . . So water, spare phone battery and they said to wear black, so that gulabi top isn't gonna wash.

. . . What, WHY?

Why are you still listening to them?!

You want me to go to the march alone?

You know what; it's fine . . . I'm just gonna go.

She looks to turn the call off. Then. . .

'Won't make a difference?'

You marched against Brexit, Trump, even with those racists at XR; but 'Black Lives Matter isn't our issue'?

Just because we've got some brown people in government doesn't mean . . . / It just proves that we've got better at being *what they want.*

We got our Oxford education . . . We know what language to speak, and it's not Gujarati – it's posh and private.

And, we both know what success tastes like and it's not shak rotli, it's organic sourdough, lemon polenta cake and a chai 'tea' latte.

Tastes good, right?

Except when that white lady got served before you?

Or when people ask: 'Where are you from, *really*?'

Or when you didn't get that job, even though you're over-qualified.

We've got so used to being oppressed that we don't even recognise when it's happening . . . Let's just 'bow our heads' and be humble, yeah?

That way, nobody can see us suffer.

Mum and Dad had so many great pieces of advice right?

'Don't make any trouble.'

Like when those kids used to throw chewing gum in my hair . . . You cut the pieces out so carefully, so Mum wouldn't know.

'Chin up', right?

The next time it happened, there was more chewing gum and it didn't end there: that one-off incident became a habit.

'Turn the other cheek'.

You cut your hair off, Sand: but they did it to you anyway.

Maybe that's why connecting to black culture was so important, right? It made us feel we weren't alone and were part of a struggle.

We listened to Michael, Jodeci and TLC . . .

But you never had any black friends.

We fancied Denzel and Will Smith.

But you stayed out of the sun, so you didn't get 'too dark' . . .

We've always been 'different', right?

When I brought James home . . . First Mum said I was too young. Then, Dad went on about the 'shame of having a Kalla in the family'. What will everyone say?!

Somebody's always at the bottom of the pile? Yeah . . .

'If we can do it, why can't they?'

If they'd just study more, work harder. Stop being violent/drug addicts/ sex addicts/misogynists/fill in random misconception.

If they'd just . . . : 'stop making trouble . . .' and just work hard.

Be more like us, and part of the solution.

I know, Sand, but James isn't any 'different', that's the point.

Deep down, there's that sense in all of us: We're better than them.

That way we're not at the bottom.

Beat as she packs her bag.

It's not our fault we get treated better, is it?

We're in the middle, put in the middle, staying in the middle; I don't know.

One part wounded, but the other part is privileged too.

So we turn the other cheek, to all of this.

Truth is, deep down, none of us have really dealt with what's being done to us.

But also, what we're doing to others.

We need to talk about this anti-blackness.

It's so deep. So knitted into who we are and our success.

. . . You know what doesn't make a difference, Sand?

Staying silent. And that's our problem, always has been.

You can keep thinking this isn't our issue.

That thinking is keeping you down, as much as it's keeping you up.

And while that still exists in your heart: They win.

They win.

When we're turning the other cheek, keeping our eyes down, we're getting no where, Sand.

We have to look up from where we are . . .

Stop being scared.

And

Fuck the middle.

First presented online by Kali Theatre in October 2020.

Social Distancing

Emteaz Hussain

A Kali SOLOS commission, originally intended for online audiences.

Fozzy (Fozia)   Sixteen. British Asian. Lives with her family. She is about to start a new Sixth Form College (UAST) to study A Levels.

To Whom   Naima. Sixteen. British Asian. Fozzy's former but now estranged best friend.

Where   Fozzy's bedroom.

Where   2020. Early September.

What has just happened   Fozzy is on her phone attempting to Facetime Naima.

Fozzy   c'mon Naima!

No answer . . .

Ends call.

Tries again . . . no answer . . . dial tone continues. . .

where are you, Naima?

Ends the call.

Beat.

Starts a voice note:

I know you're there, Naima . . .

ma cuzzy, she's seen you down Heavenly Desserts with that refugee girl last Tuesday . . .

I know you aint in Telford with your fifty million relatives like you do every summer, y'know, leaving me on my ones

call me . . . will ya . . .

Ends voice note.

Later/next day/a week later. Naima calling back. Fozzy, eager, picks up:

Fozzy   Naima – where you been?

course I wanna go with you

no I'm not going Emmanuel's?

no, it was one of my options, well, UAST does business as well as my other subjects. . . I know it doesn't do media, but I'm gonna drop it, do computer science, so I got business, computer science, sociology . . . just need 2 Bs and a C for uni, that's it!

Mum's happier, well, she preferred Emmanuel High, but then I told her I got more friends at UAST so . . . she was cool, ennit.

you thought I was going with Tara and Keisha to Emmanuel's? no way!

is that what I said?!

can't remember saying that!

what do you mean I beg them as friends . . . that's not true, Naima . . . I never hang out with them more than you . . .

so, y'wanna meet at the bus stop or what? this Monday? go together? I know you'll be there that time, 7.40, cos Adeel'll be on the bus, and we both know, I mean – correction - we all know what y'going to be doing with Adeel, don't we?

raaaaah!

how you'd get that bus every morning for school and you'd be like forty-five minutes early, just to stare at him . . . he dint even know did he? like you were so low key, discreet, got to respect ya' for that!

even though all of 11C knew . . .

no one's gonna ever forget when Mr Herman the German shouted '11C detention at break!' with his big skanky breath spraying us all . . . then your voice echoes round the classroom – 'I 'WANNA SNOG ADEEL MALIK!'

Beat.

then total silence

Oh! My! Days! the shame of it! behsti man!

even 'Herman the German' dropped his whiteboard marker dint he? then everyone stared cos everyone thought that you were just so quiet, and like good dint they? even I was shocked!

that's when Tara and Keisha came to me at break and said, that was the most embarrassing thing ever . . . cos you was pretending to be something you're not . . .

Beat.

but they don't know you like I know ya' do they?

then they said that they hate fake people but, how 'I'm alright', and why do I hang out with . . .

but it's always been me n' you since year 7, hiding out together in the end cubicle cos we didn't want to see anyone . . . that was bare jokes!!

Beat.

did I say that?

you might be getting confused?

you're my bestie not them, they're just y'know . . .

you're going with the refugee girl on Monday?!

I know she has a name

I don't mind her . . . Khartoon,

yeah she's cool, we'll all go together won't we?

I'll be there anyway on the bus and kasme I won't say anything to Adeel...he doesn't know anything anyway cos that was all in your head, wasn't it . . . raaaah! promise, won't say anything if I see him – wallahi fam!

what?

he's left for uni?

oh.

I dint know

that's cos I ant seen you for ages, we ant had our chats, have we? been time Naima! where y'been . . . ?

Beat.

you saw it!?

they said no one saw it,

it was jus' jokes . . . that's all . . .

just they asked me to the park – if I'll be part of their bubble, and you weren't getting in touch. we were having this picnic – social distancing – I went to Costcutter, spent five pounds on three packs of Doritos.

the posh ones.

what do you mean I only bought you Smart Price ones?

it was a celebration, lockdown relaxing. I bought three packs of Doritos, nicked a bottle of vodka from my brothers' bedroom, and got a packet of strawberry laces, y'know the pound pack we always get and share

I walked to the park, it was hot under my mask n' I thought about Amma lecturing me to socially distance but y'know what . . . it didn't look like people were, an' I just thought they're in their bubbles, just like I was with Tara, Keisha and all their friends, we were jus' going to be like this big bubble hanging out all summer, together, cos y'know it's Tara and Keisha and they know like everyone, don't they?

I was waiting, lookin' at that big tree, y'know by that big oak tree

sent a message to the group – they said they were on their way, just got held up cos Keisha needs a face mask

so, I sat by the tree, took some pics of the cloud formations. there was that one that looked like the Imam's face . . . sent it you . . . you never got back, could see you saw it though, then I heard something in the bush, thought it was them

but it was just this like big raven.

made me think of you in your oversized black jumper and your long black skirt that got bigger and bigger every year – I did tell ya' to tell your mum that your cousins' uniforms are too big for ya dint I? . . .

at least we don't have to wear them anymore . . .

what do ya mean?

I sat with you in 'philosophy and ethics' . . . no, that wasn't cos they didn't take that subject, that's cos you're my bestie . . .

I was waiting for forty-five minutes and they weren't here yet, I'd eaten a pack of Doritos and drank half a bottle of vodka . . . and then I was sick by that big oak tree.

you coulda told me you seen the pics?

everyone?

everyone from school saw?

Tara told me they were behind that big bush watching me, told me I was hilarious . . . got snaps of me on my ones, that it was so funny . . . even got a snap of me vomming by the tree

'it's only on Snapchat, don't worry, they're deleted, cross my heart and hope to die.'

so I walked home on my ones, when I got in Amma asked if I'd kept my social distance from my friends and I said yeah, Mum, I did, then she asked me if I'd been crying, I said no, just hay fever, Mum . . . y'know what mums are like . . .

Beat.

it's cool – everything's been deleted . . .

haven't seen or heard from any of them after that, I unfollowed all their accounts

Beat.

no need to be there 7.40?

you'll see me at the bus stop 8.15?

Beat.

oh yeah!

First presented online by Kali Theatre in December 2020

Educating Britain

Alia Bano

A Kali SOLOS commission, originally intended for online audiences.

Fatimah Khan   Late thirties. British Asian. Muslim. Teacher. Mother of two children – Idris and Raif.

To Whom   Online group.

Where   Fatimah's home.

When   2020. Term time. Weekday. Just after 9 a.m.

What Has Just Happened   Fatimah Khan, in her pyjamas picking up books. A laptop on her table, she is talking into a camera set up which we do not see. She will be addressing that audience directly unless stage directions indicate otherwise.

Fatimah   So, some of you asked me how am I doing it? Well, here it is warts and all. One sec . . .

(*To her kids, offstage.*) Idris, Raif, you had better have started that work I gave you and make sure you don't disturb me for the next forty minutes or there will be no iPads for the next month.

The irony of being a teacher and not being able to teach your own kids.

Dumps the books on a table. One of which must be Hamlet.

Fuck . . . fuck. I'm late. (*Puts a blazer over her PJs and ties a scarf around her neck.*) At least the head can't walk in and go on about punctuality. There are some advantages to lockdown.

(*To her laptop.*) Good morning, year 10. Let's get back to studying tragedies.

Seems like quite an appropriate topic with everything that's going on.

Fucking typical! All they have to do is roll over and switch on their computer or phone which they're usually glued to at every other moment but to actually try and get them to log into a lesson.

(*To the laptop.*) Hello, Mina, I didn't see you there. Do you want to continue reading *Hamlet* while we wait for the others to log on?

Even in the midst of hell, there's always one . . . one kid trying to scrabble out of the lost paradise that is Sherwood High. Mina Patel, a gold star in a dark sky.

It's pupils like that that give you hope and make you want the system to work. Kids like that and obviously my own rugrats.

(*To laptop.*) 'Something is rotten in the state of Denmark.' That's a great quote, Mina.

And it's the fucking education system.

(*To laptop.*) Why don't you analyse it? Owen, what time do you call this? Yes, I know it's 9.15; You're fifteen minutes late. Mina can you please work with Owen to answer the questions on the PowerPoint.

That's the thing with this job – all anyone goes on about is the long holidays; it's a fucking fallacy.

You have marking, planning or reading up on some new hare-brained idea the government has to solve, another societal problem because there's no real plan. Terrorism . . . teachers, shit parents . . . teachers, bad behaviour . . . teachers, pandemic . . . teachers.

It's always the fucking teachers! What other sector gets suckered into solving all the woes of the world? Certainly not Parliament, they couldn't organise a piss-up in a brewery.

And when schools do have to close, every fucking parent in the country goes into meltdown. If you can't cope with your lovely darling for a few weeks, imagine how we feel having to look after thirty of them for forty weeks. You suddenly begin to understand why Nurse Ratched was the way she was.

That was a reference to *One Flew over the Cuckoo's Nest* for those of you who hated English at school, or if you're Generation Z or a Millennial and can only concentrate if someone is TikToking about something. I guess progress has to happen, (*sings The Buggles'*) 'Video killed the radio star.'

I'm beginning to think there's no salary worth this. A few Saturdays ago, I was in Aldi. I started to feel envious of the cashiers as they scanned and I packed my fruit and veg away. It's a hard job, you can see it, but at least when they clock off, they clock off. That rarely happens with teaching. (*Breaks into song.*) 'It's always on my mind. It's always on my mind.'

As I was walking out, there was this job advert, 'Become a manager for Aldi'. The salary 45 bags, 45K if you're not down with the latest lingo. A teacher working for ten years wouldn't see that. And if some arsehole is rude to them, they can chuck them out or if they get physically violent, they can ban them. A teacher wouldn't get that. Ofsted will fail a school if they exclude too many kids. Fail the school, not the parents, not the kid but collective punishment for all the teachers doing everybody else's jobs but their own.

Do you know the definition of teaching? Have you actually sat down and looked it up?

Teaching is the concerted sharing of knowledge and experience, which is usually organised within a discipline, the provision of stimulus to the psychological and intellectual growth of a person by another person or artefact.

I'm not sure anyone has really done that since the nineties. (*Beat.*) I wanted to be a teacher because I wanted to be Robin Williams in *Dead Poets Society* and that's the power and danger of a good story ladies and gents.

School's become a glorified babysitting club at its least and at its most it's a device to ensure control of the masses. The rich opt out with fee-paying schools while ensuring they have a good supply of serfs.

(*To laptop.*) Yes, Mina, why didn't Hamlet take action earlier? Bloody excellent question, Mina. Why don't you think about that?

Why don't we all think about it? Why does Hamlet act so fucking late? Because even though he's Danish, he was written by a Brit. And us Brits are best at doing nothing when we should be up in arms, and rebelling at the way everything is in a mess, but we're just a bunch of Hamlets, all whinge and no action.

(*To laptop.*) Owen, why haven't you written anything?

Because it's boring! I'm sorry the most famous writer in the world isn't entertaining you, Owen, as he has everyone else for the last 500 years.

(*To laptop.*) You need to write something. (*Beat.*) For your GCSEs, to help you get a good college or get a job.

He has a plan to be famous. Thanks reality TV for making celebrities out of stupid people and making our jobs ten times harder!

(*To laptop.*) Sorry, Owen?

I think I've underestimated Owen Richards. That's the most insightful comment he's made in class for a while. He just said (mimics Owen) 'It must suck being a teacher. I'd never be stupid enough to be a teacher.'

And there is the real tragedy. Owen Richards, who cannot write a word without a capital letter in the middle, has already realised at the tender age of fourteen years and five months something that I've only just come to realise at my not so tender age, that no one of a sound mind would be a teacher in today's world. At least not in the state sector. Because for each gold star, there are a thousand dark skies: from the kids, to the parents, to the senior leaders and let's not forget the government.

She closes her laptop and smiles.

That's why I'm quitting. I start my new job as manager of Aldi next month.

Blackout.

First presented online by Kali Theatre in November 2020.

Me and Ed

Atiha Sen Gupta

A Kali SOLOS commission, originally intended for online audiences.

Chandra   Early twenties. From Bristol. British Asian/Caribbean.
An activist.

To Whom   A journalist making a film.

Where   Bristol.

When   2020. June.

What Has Just Happened   Chandra is part of a group of Bristol's Black
Lives Matter activists who have pulled down the statue of Edward Colston
(the seventeenth-century Bristolian slave trader). They have daubed him in
red paint and thrown him into Bristol Harbour as part of nationwide
protests at the way in which black lives have been systematically attacked
and undermined. Some of the group of protestors have also been arrested.
Here Chandra explains to a journalist why she did it.

Chandra *looks down at the ground, still, silent, statuesque. Suddenly she
is animated and looks into the camera.*

Chandra   We good to go?

I was five when I first met Ed.

My first day at school.

My first memory.

Hand in hand with Mum and Dad. Insisting they both swing me for the
umpteenth time and make the 'wee' sound. The 'wee' sound was
obligatory. Mum saying grown-up girls keep their feet on the ground,
Dad disagreeing – looking at me apologetically and slipping me a
Werther's Original to keep me sweet.

And there he was.

Looking down on us, on me.

Hair curling around his shoulders. A hand cupping a weary chin. The other holding a walking stick.

I looked up and asked, 'Who's he?'

Mum and Dad looked at each other:

'Who's going to tell her?'

*

School was . . . interesting.

After the initial "What's your name?" "How many sisters and brothers do you have?" "What's your favourite colour?", the conversation progressed to "Where are you from?"

Of course I wanted to say 'Here', but even then I knew the real answer lay elsewhere. I went home and asked Mum and Dad.

The next day I strode in.

(*Proudly.*) 'The Caribbean.'

The kid's face fell.

'You can't be from the Caribbean – you're not black.'

I didn't know what to say to this so after school I trotted back to the rents.

Mum said I was black; that we were black on account of us not being white:

'Black is a political colour.'

'What's "political"?'

Dad looked at Mum:

'One thing at a time.'

Mum rolled her eyes.

'It's not only black people who live in the Caribbean – but Indians – like us.'

'But Pooja in Blue Class is Indian and from India. How can an Indian not be from India?'

Mum said: 'You know how we talked about slavery?'

(*Almost an aside.*) Yeah – dinner times were fun at my house.

'When slavery ended, they created a new system to replace it called indentured labour. Instead of Africans, they were Asians.'

Needless to say, when I reported my findings the next day, the kids were somewhat unimpressed.

The next time I was asked where I was from, I said India and that settled it.

*

When I reached secondary school, the boys started asking each other:

'Do you prefer blondes or brunettes?'

They would answer accordingly and then high five each other on their preferences. I marvelled at their ability to exclude me without excluding me.

Word got round that one of the girls from my class was selling dodgy contact lenses in the common room – green, blue, hazel – all yours for a fiver. I went hungry that lunchtime – abandoned my belly and bought myself a new set of eyes.

I opted for blue – believing I could buy myself out of my brownness. I didn't realise it at the time but she didn't have a single white girl as a customer.

Contacts in, school done, homeward bound; through my blue-tinted glasses, I spotted Ed and wondered what colour eyes he had. Surely blue? Green at a push.

Normally I would always remember to take my contacts out before getting home. This one time, though, I forgot. Mum was home early from work.

She looks at me, looks away, then looks at me again.

'What's that?'

She comes closer.

'Nothing.'

'Your eyes . . .'

Her eyes widen as she realises what I have done – how I have erased her, how I have erased us.

Her hand rises and makes its way across my cheek. Crisp.

The force of it actually caused one of my contacts to fall out.

'Do you know how hard your father and I worked to pave the way for you to be yourself?'

My eyes watered.

Mum immediately apologised.

Dad didn't talk to her for a month.

And I never wore contacts again.

*

I started reading – online, offline.

I talked to people, asked questions, listened, argued, listened again.

Opted for History A level. All the usual clichés apply – if you don't know where you're coming from, you can't know where you're going.

I learnt about Ed.

100,000 wrenched from their homes. 100,000 branded with the initials RAC on their chests. Hot metal on cold skin.

I must have passed Ed thousands of times – twice a day for thirteen years – and he went from being part of the furniture to being a splinter in my skin.

And each time I passed, there was something new.

Pigeon poo, piss on his pedestal, chips and curry sauce.

But do you know what the thing with Ed was?

Nothing stuck.

All the poo, piss and chips could be, would be washed away and then he'd be back to new.

Fresh as a daisy.

Good as gold.

Bright as bronze.

It's like a superpower, isn't it? Some people can do anything, like anything, and it just slips right off them. Nothing sticks.

*

It's basic physics – you know this – what goes up, must come down. Whether that's an apple falling from a tree or a coin you toss to make a life decision or . . .

Him.

It.

Ed.

No one and nothing is exempt from gravity.

People are saying we did what we did because we are brutes who do not understand history but actually it's the opposite – we know too much. We understand everything.

Never underestimate the power of newly discovered knowledge, a face mask and a rope.

*

You might say, 'But he was a man of his time . . .'

But he's not a man of ours.

She looks directly into the camera.

I didn't want to live under his shadow anymore.

Does that answer your question?

First presented online by Kali Theatre in November 2020.

The Duologues

Song for a Sanctuary

Rukhsana Ahmad

Kamla Thirty. A refuge worker. Working-class. A Caribbean Indian, from South London. Educated but doesn't speak any Indian languages.

Rajinder Late thirties. A Sikh from the Punjab in North India. Middle class. She has three children.

Where The refuge office.

When Daytime.

What Has Just Happened Rajinder fled her abusive husband and sought refuge at her own initiative. Normally, a woman is referred by a doctor, social worker or the police. However, Rajinder, who's a strict conformist, did not wish to involve the authorities. This refusal to follow the normal protocols has angered Rajinder's case worker, Kamla, a radical feminist. Despite their shared Indian heritage, there is a vast gulf between the two women to do with faith, politics and culture. They clashed from the outset and continue to do so.

Kamla *is speaking on the telephone to* **Katie** *in the refuge office.*

Kamla Now listen, Katie, you'll get worse sleeping rough like that. We'll have you soon as we have a place . . . Why don't you put Bev on the phone, I'll speak to her she'll get you fixed up for a few days . . . See you soon.

Enter **Rajinder**.

Kamla Won't keep you a moment.

Rajinder *sits.*

Kamla Bev, we can't offer her a room for a couple of weeks yet . . . Can you have her for now? . . . Wonderful, I'll speak to you very soon. . . . Okay. Bye now.

Pause.

Kamla Sorry about that.

Rajinder   That's all right.

Kamla   Tea? Coffee?

Rajinder   No, thanks.

Kamla   Well, how are things?

Rajinder   Not too bad.

Kamla   Good, good.

Pause.

Kamla   What about school? Are they all settled?

Rajinder   Yes. They seem happy enough.

Kamla   Finances? Everything running smoothly?

Rajinder   It's alright, at the moment.

Kamla   So, no problems at all?

Pause.

What am I saying? Of course there are problems. Dumb question. I mean any problems to do with the refuge, with other residents, or with facilities?

Rajinder   Sharing a house isn't easy, even with your own family sometimes there are problems. There's been a few, but only little little ones. I'm managing.

Kamla   Good. Great to hear that.

Pause.

Have you thought of some training for yourself?

Rajinder   I got a BA in India. You can't do much with it out here.

Kamla   So what've you thought about doing?

Pause.

Rajinder   Horoscopes . . . I mean professionally. I could do that from home, charge people, it would fit in with the children's timings.

Kamla   You can't make enough doing that.

Rajinder   That depends on what you call enough, and on your luck.

Kamla   You can't believe in all that seriously! It leaves no room for human effort. How can you ask people to work towards change if you believe that someone else is pulling the strings?

Rajinder   It doesn't mean you can't choose . . . just that . . . the circumstances in which you have to make your choices are often beyond your own control. Like birth, or death.

Kamla   Hmm. I hadn't thought of it like that. (*Pause.*) But there's a real world out there; you need a certain minimum to survive. Might be useful to retrain in more practical terms, hmm? Now, how did it go with the housing officer today?

Rajinder   Not very well, I'm afraid.

Kamla   Any special reason?

Rajinder   It wasn't so much what he said . . . it's . . . what I couldn't say. I hadn't realised, until today that . . . you . . . have to go through all that to get a place. I've decided I can't take that.

Kamla   What! You can't afford to decide those things any more.

Rajinder   What do you mean? It's my life we're talking about. I'm not one of your illiterate working-class women to be managed by you.

Kamla   Well, that's how it's done whatever class you are. You've got to establish your need to separate from your husband, that's all.

Rajinder   I've to explain to some stranger the history of fifteen years of marriage, expose every intimate detail of my life – and you say, 'that's all', *haan*?

But then you wouldn't know about it.

Kamla   It's not pleasant, or easy, I know, but that is the procedure, for everyone, regardless of race and religion.

Rajinder   I see.

Kamla   In any case, you don't have to feel ashamed of anything. The shame's all his.

Rajinder   Are you married, Kamla?

Kamla   No. Fortunately. What's that got to do with anything?

Rajinder   How can you understand what's involved then?

Kamla   With respect, I can see marriage, as an institution, without the rose-coloured glasses.

Rajinder   Aren't we allowed to have privacy any more just because we left our homes?

Kamla   What's the big deal in privacy?

Rajinder   It's important to me.

Kamla   Don't you see, the privatisation of women's lives keeps us from seeing domestic violence in a socio-political context.

Rajinder   Leave out the analysis! I've got to deal with my life as I think best.

Kamla   Your story is common enough, believe me. It's part of a pattern: of how men have used women over the years. That's why we started the support group sessions. You haven't been to any of those yet, have you?

Rajinder   I don't believe in washing my dirty linen in public. Thank you

Kamla   There's something positive about sharing your experiences.

Rajinder   Sharing your troubles seems more like a sign of weakness to me.

Kamla   Perhaps if you try a session some time . . .

Rajinder   I don't think you understand my language, Kamla. I didn't marry in a registry office. I married before God. It wasn't just a social arrangement it was a sacred bond, made with body and soul.

Kamla   Something broke that bond for you and exposing that something now is part of the price you pay for your release.

Rajinder   What do I want release for? I'm not going to marry anyone else. I just left, because . . .

Pause.

Kamla   Because . . .?

Rajinder   . . . there was no other way.

Kamla   I'm sorry, I know it still hurts.

Pause.

Rajinder I need time to think through things.

Kamla Time goes by, women forget the hurt, their wounds begin to heal and they start imagining things might get better, if they go back. That seems easiest if you don't have accommodation.

Rajinder I've done my going back. I won't make the same mistake again, you'll see. And I won't take a begging bowl to anyone. I can survive.

Kamla It's not begging. You have a right to housing. You need a place to live and a proper source of income. You're living in bloody cloud-cuckoo land. I weep inside if one of my women returns to a violent marriage. I feel as if I've failed her.

Rajinder Strange – this passion you put into destroying other people's marriages. All that matters to you is that I should never go back!

Kamla You're still hankering for some woolly romantic dream of saving your marriage with your heroism. Can't you see there's nothing left for me to destroy? You ran away to hide from that awful shell of a relationship that you can't even speak about to others . . .

Rajinder I don't need to.

Exit **Rajinder**. **Kamla** *gets up and paces.*

Kamla Stupid fool!

First presented by Kali Theatre in October 1991 at the Lyric Hammersmith, Birmingham Rep Studio and on tour.

Calcutta Kosher

Shelley Silas

Mozelle Seventies. Indian Jewish. Widowed with three daughters. Mozelle is the matriarch of the family and has recently suffered a debilitating heart attack. Mozelle lies in a wicker day chair, a blanket half covering her. She wears an old dress and several gaudy necklaces and three gold churies (bangles) on her wrist.

Esther Late forties. Mozelle's eldest daughter. Now lives in the UK and is married to Peter with two children. Esther wears a simple, dark blue dress, a sensible hat and low-heeled open-toe shoes. Everything about her is practical.

Where India, Calcutta. The ground-floor room of a crumbling house. A brass ceiling fan remains stationary throughout. A couple of pieces of old furniture – including a large wooden mantlepiece clock and some morahs – are placed around the room. Doors at the back of the stage lead to a veranda. Just visible outside is the stump of a tree. There is a large black and white photo of the Victoria Memorial on the back wall with a few family photos

When October. Friday (Shabbat). Late afternoon.

What Has Just Happened Mozelle has called her daughters (Esther and Silvie) back to the family home in Calcutta to explain her will and more significantly to reveal her closely held secret that they have in fact another sister (Maki) who will be the daughter to inherit the house on her death. Before she dies Mozelle is intent on telling Esther and Silvie the truth about her passionate love affair with Maki's father (Ravi) whilst married to their father. When Esther and Silvie moved abroad, Maki moved in to take care of Mozelle, ostensibly as her 'housekeeper', and no one suspected the truth of their relationship. This extract is near the beginning of the play and Esther is the first to arrive, oblivious as yet to the 'secret' but shocked by her mother's ill health. She is in the entrance of the room and staring at her mother, taking in the sight before her.

Mozelle   It's alright. I'm still alive.

She opens her arms to **Esther**. **Esther** *walks up to* **Mozelle**, *hugs her.*

Mozelle   It's good to see you, Esther.

Esther   And you.

Mozelle   It's been a few years since you were here.

Esther   A few.

Mozelle   Ten I think. But who's counting?

***

Esther   I'd forgotten how quickly the dust gets into your body.

Beat.

Mozelle   Don't you have dust in London? How do I look?

Esther   I'm not sure.

Mozelle   You're not sure? You haven't seen me for two years. How do I look? Do I look the same?

Esther   You look pale.

Mozelle   Do I look sick?

Esther   You look sick.

Mozelle   Then say so. How are my grandchildren and Peter? How is Peter?

Esther   Fine, everyone is fine. They all send their love.

Mozelle   And kisses?

Esther   What?

Mozelle   Kisses. Did they send kisses?

Esther   Of course.

Mozelle   Give them to me.

Esther (*reluctantly*)   This is from Amy. And this is from Alice.

Mozelle   What about Peter?

Esther   Peter sends a kiss too.

Mozelle *offers her cheek to* **Esther**. **Esther** *kisses her quickly.*

Esther *is not the most affectionate or tactile woman.*

Mozelle   Just one?

Esther *kisses her mother again.*

Mozelle   That's better. Let me look at you.

Mozelle *examines* **Esther**.

Mozelle   You put on weight.

Esther   A bit.

Mozelle   A lot.

Esther   A pound or two.

Mozelle   More than that.

***

Esther (*beat*)   So what's wrong?

Mozelle   I had a heart attack.

Esther   A heart attack!

Mozelle   But here I am, dear. Alive and well. Ready to have some fun with my daughters.

Esther   A heart attack? What do you mean a heart attack?

Mozelle   I didn't want to worry you.

Esther   You think we weren't worried?

Mozelle   You know how excitable Silvie is. And flying can be no fun these days, with so much security and *pagla* (mad) people who want the world to end.

Esther   You should have said. You should have told us.

***

Mozelle   Do you make our food at home?

Esther   Why?

Mozelle   Your weight. Our food is full of calories.

Esther   The girls are too fussy.

Mozelle   Too spoilt.

Esther   And Peter likes his food plain.

Mozelle   Ashkenazie. (*Beat.*) Does he like chicken soup?

Esther   Sometimes.

Mozelle   You should make him pish pash.

Esther   He calls it baby food.

Mozelle   I suppose he likes egg and chips? Sunny side up.

Esther   Not always.

Mozelle   Tomato sauce?

Esther   Occasionally.

Mozelle   It is the devil's blood.

Esther   It's not that bad.

Mozelle   Fish balls?

Esther   Of course.

Mozelle   I didn't know fish had them.

She laughs to herself.

***

Esther   Are you alright?

Mozelle   *Asi dasi.* (So, so.)

Esther   Are you going to be alright?

Mozelle   Who knows?

Esther   Has Dr Chuck prescribed anything?

Mozelle   There's nothing left to prescribe. I have my pills. If I take any more I'll shake rattle and roll all the way to my grave.

Esther   What would you say if I wanted to take you home?

Mozelle   Home?

Esther   Yes.

Mozelle   To your home?

Esther   That's right.

Mozelle   London?

Esther *nods.*

Mozelle   This is my home. This is where I belong.

Esther   There's nothing here for you. Every one's either moved on . . . or died.

Mozelle   Not true. There's still Alfred and Seema. You should have seen Alfred's face when I told him you and Silvie were coming. Lit up like the Victoria Memorial on independence day.

Esther   It's hardly a community.

Mozelle   They come here once a week and we play Towli or Carrom. And I win every time. When we are together we look around the room and we remember the old days. You should see us. Three old buddies. Last year they took me to Gopalpur for a holiday. I sent you a postcard. Did you get it?

Esther   No.

Mozelle   A camel walking across the desert is faster than the post in that damn place. They are such junglies. Behind with the times. Calcutta is the only place to live in India you know.

Esther   What about Bombay?

Mozelle   Too damn noisy.

Esther   It isn't exactly quiet in Calcutta.

Mozelle   This is where I was born and this is where I will die.

Esther   You want to die here? All alone?

Mozelle   I have Maki. Your dadi is buried here. And Ravi's ashes were scattered in the river.

Esther   Ravi?

Mozelle   Maki's dadi. I like to be near them both.

Esther   We can make you more comfortable.

Mozelle   Who is this 'we'?

Esther   Me and Peter. The girls would love it. You'll have your own space, anything you need.

Mozelle   A smelly old woman like me?

Esther   You don't smell.

Mozelle   Usually I do. But Maki hasn't let me eat garlic for weeks so now it's not so bad.

Esther   You've been eating garlic?

Mozelle   Great thick pieces. It keeps away the vampires. And clears my blood. But she said it stinks too much so now I don't eat it.

Esther   I really want you to consider coming home with me.

Mozelle   I will not leave my synagogues. Every Friday night, Faisal arranges prayers at one of them. But you know, I don't think we'll make it tonight. I feel a little tired.

Pause.

Esther   I want you to think about it, Molly. You're so far away from us.

Mozelle   You're the one who's far away.

Esther   Nothing's changed.

Mozelle   Maybe not in this house, but Calcutta is more modern than you think. Maki tells me that if you phone to find the time of a train in England, you will speak to someone in Calcutta. Calcutta is where I belong.

Esther   But there's nothing here for you now.

Mozelle   What will I do in London? Watch television, go to the theatre? Eat your English food with no spices?

Esther   We have spices. We can go out for an Indian any time you like. Or Italian, or whatever you want.

Mozelle   No.

Esther   Just listen.

Mozelle   No.

Esther   I've spoken to Peter. We want you to come home. With me.

Mozelle   And die among strangers?

First presented by Kali Theatre in February 2004 year at Southwark Playhouse and on tour in a co-production with Tara Arts. In June 2004 this production was presented by Theatre Royal Stratford East. It was revived for Kali's twenty-first birthday in 2012 at the Arcola Theatre.

Bells

Yasmin Whittaker-Khan

Pepsi Twenty-seven. London-born transvestite from Indian Sikh parentage. Wears fitted bootleg trousers, fitted t-shirts with logos printed on them and funky trainers. He has long hair tied in a ponytail or plait. During the day he wears light make-up and for the club nights he wears female dress and lots of make-up and jewellery. Doesn't smoke, drinks and sniffs poppers.

Aiesha Twenty. Dancer. Born and brought up in Pakistan. Wears glamorous tight-fitting salwar kameez suits, lots of make-up and jewellery. Doesn't smoke but drinks whisky. She is a practising Muslim.

Where East London. The play is set in a South Asian courtesan club (Bells) which is above a butcher's shop. The audience are treated as club members. Before the performance each member of the audience is given a wad of fake money which they can spend if they wish at Bells during the dance performances.

When 2005. Early evening.

What Has Just Happened Aiesha is in a towel, grooming herself with perfumes and oils. Pepsi is also in a towel, sitting holding a hand mirror plucking his eyebrows. Funky Lollywood tunes are playing in the background. They are both giggling and singing along to the music. Aiesha is practising her dance routines. They are preparing for the evening's performance.

Pepsi and Aiesha *Tenu sajde karan noon jee kar da pir sooch di ah tu khuda te nahee* (I feel like bowing down and worshipping you but then I think you're not God) *teray baj marun nu jee kar da, pir sooch di ah tu jooda te nahee* (I feel like dying in your arms but then I think maybe you're too distant for me) . . .

Pepsi No, no jump up a bit more. Shake your tits. Look, like this.

Aiesha I was

Pepsi Move your hips and make me want to fuck you.

Aiesha   Jaani I'm good but not that good. I doubt that I'll ever be able to make you . . . want to fuck me.

Pepsi   Miracles have happened before.

Aiesha   Aye a miracle happens here every night.

Pepsi   Yes and we create those miracles.

Aiesha (*sarcastically*)   Now, now, it's not just us creating miracles. Madam does her fair share too?

Pepsi   The only miracle she performs is with the dregs at the end of the night.

Aiesha   Hey, those dregs, they feel they're getting a bargain and we all like a bargain . . . plus she feels like she's a wanted woman.

Pepsi   Pppfff! What're you wearing tonight?

Aiesha   Don't know yet.

Pepsi   I think . . . a boob-tube number.

Aiesha   Ooh I say Jaani.

Pepsi   I'm gonna put that new belly ring in that we bought today. Talking of today, when we're out shopping, you can stop all this bumping into blokes . . . customers . . . and chatting rubbish. I'm supposed to be keeping an eye on you, don't make my life difficult.

Aiesha (*sheepishly ignoring him*)   Belly ring . . . Well in that case, Jaani, you should wax your belly cos that won't do!

Pepsi   Do you think it's that hairy? I thought I might get away with it?

Aiesha   Oh, did you now? (*She pushes him softly.*) Lie back?

Pepsi   I know what you were up to today . . .

Aiesha   What?

Pepsi   Well . . . when we're out, don't try to sneak off?

Aiesha *in cheery, passive-aggressive mode, brings over the wax strips, gets* **Pepsi** *to lay down and she starts to wax around his belly and hips.*

Aaaaaahhhhhhhhh! Fuck!

Aiesha   Pepsi, *jaani*, when was the last time you got your bikini line done?

Pepsi   Couple of weeks ago . . . aaaaahhhhhhhhh! Man! Can't you be gentle!

Aiesha   Like hell you did. These bastards are creeping up thick and fast. Better be careful before your little soldier gets all tangled up in there. You won't be able to pee let alone do anything else.

Pepsi   Yuck shut up. You're gross. Ssssssiiiiiiiiii! Aaaahhhhh! Si! I'll go shopping without you, you know . . . and I'll choose your outfits.

She examines his navel closer and then grabs the tweezers off him and starts to pluck hairs that she might have missed.

Aiesha   Really?

Pepsi   Ouch! Ooooh! Ouch! Be careful, don't pull my knob off.

Aiesha   I'll try not to. But I can't even see it at the moment.

Pepsi   That's cos it's not for you to look at.

Aiesha   Excuse me.

Pepsi   Well, girlfriend, my meat is destined for higher things in life.

Aiesha   What Ashraf's shitty bottom. Here, you're done!

Pepsi (*sarcastically*)   Cheers, girlfriend . . . (*Afterthought.*) My Ashraf's bottom is as juicy and soft as a peach.

Aiesha   You mean a shrivelled peach. What do you see in him?

They both start to put on their make-up.

Pepsi (*points the mirror at his navel*)   What do you mean?

Aiesha   You know what I mean.

Pepsi   I love him.

Aiesha   A dirty old man?

Pepsi   No different to the dirty old men you shag.

Aiesha   Yes but I'm not in love with them.

Pepsi   You've got a rock not a heart.

Aiesha   Ooh listen to you . . . all high and mighty!

Pepsi   Look, I might not be into books and things like you, but I know a good thing.

Aiesha   Tell me, Pepsi, what's a good thing?

Pepsi   You know what I mean. (*Takes off his towel to put on his corset, whilst carefully tucking his penis back and starts to put on a strapless* *bra stuffed with silicone gel pads to give him a bit of a cleavage.*) Like my body for instance. (*Laughs.*) That's a good thing!

Aiesha   No I don't know what you mean . . . a good thing?! . . . Come here, let me sort your petticoat out. Tuck your soldier in a bit more, I can see a slight lump.

Pepsi   Oops!

Aiesha   So what do you mean? A good thing?

Pepsi   Listen, let's chat when you're not so close to my dick?

Aiesha   Why're you worried that I might turn you on?

Pepsi   No!

Aiesha   Don't you trust me?

Pepsi   Yeah I do.

Aiesha   What is it then?

Pepsi   What do you mean?

Aiesha   Why is it you jump up whenever madam or Ashraf click their fingers?

She starts taking off her towel and starts to get dressed by putting on sexy underwear and a gloriously sequined and embroidered Langah (long flowing skirt) with a tight-fitting sari blouse. They both help each other get dressed.

Pepsi   No I don't.

Aiesha   Yes . . . we can all live in denial.

Pepsi   I'm not the one in denial.

Aiesha   Really?

Pepsi   You think you're too high and mighty. Ashraf makes me feel real. I can be who I am with him. I don't have to pretend.

Aiesha   Course you do. Look at you . . . If that isn't pretence then what is?

Pepsi   I tell you this is a performance. Just like you perform.

Aiesha   Let's not argue . . . there's better out there for us.

Pepsi   Just because you've been with madam since you were thirteen doesn't mean you've missed out on anything.

Aiesha Haven't I?

Pepsi I've been out there and the world is a bastard to the likes of you and me . . . really it is.

Aiesha I'm not like you.

Pepsi You are to 'the world'.

Aiesha What world? The world of Bells or the world of humans?

Pepsi Do you really think people are gonna believe that you're an educated Pathan from Peshawar or a two-bit whore who chose this profession.

First presented by Kali Theatre in March 2005 at Birmingham Repertory Theatre, Southwark Playhouse and on tour.

Deadeye

Amber Lone

Deema   Eighteen. British Asian. Lives at home with her parents. Attends college.

Tariq   Twenty-two. Deema's older brother and a drug addict. Slight build. Tariq wears a battered hooded raincoat which is too big for him and under which he has too many clothes.

Where   Inner-city street.

When   Early evening.

What Has Just Happened   Deema is a loving sister to her brother Tariq, but Tariq is mixing with the wrong crowd. Tariq is a drug addict, his supplier is Jimmy, their cousin. In the previous scene, Jimmy threatened Deema. He accused Tariq of stealing from him and is hunting him down to get his money back. Deema worries about her brother's behaviour and feels the stress of her parents struggling to pay bills and keep a roof over their heads, particularly when their father is a fantasist and refuses to look clearly at their parlous financial situation. This scene is the first time Deema has seen Tariq in a few days. Deema is carrying a bag of groceries. Tariq walks past.

Deema   Oi

Tariq *jumps.*

Tariq   Fuck's sake . . . what are you doin' here?

Deema   I was passin'.

Tariq   You flippin' following' me?

Deema   Said I was passin' and I needed to talk to you.

Tariq   You're going on like some sort of nutter. I'm alright.

Deema   No you're not.

Tariq   We'll talk about it later, right.

He stops to lean against a wall.

Deema   We can't talk about it later.

Tariq   Please, man . . . my legs are killin' me.

Deema   Jimmy said he hadn't seen ya. Mom and Dad . . . we've got some trouble at home.

Tariq   Aaah! Fuck.

Deema   What is wrong with you?

Tariq   Legs are hurting . . . like someone's driven over 'em with a truck.

Deema *leans next to him and starts to roll a cigarette.*

Tariq   Can I have one?

Deema *passes him the rolled-up cigarette.* **Tariq** *takes a drag and bends over then tries to stretch, all the time acting as if he's dying.* **Deema** *is motionless.*

Deema   It's your own doing.

Tariq   Need your help . . . I'm desperate.

Deema   You're always desperate. Meanwhile I go to college, apply for jobs, get the shopping in, help pay the bills, wash the dishes, make the roti . . . tell Dad lies about where you are . . .

Tariq   Didn't ask you to. Did I ask you?

Deema   This got delivered yesterday. I didn't want to give it to him.

She hands **Tariq** *a letter and he reads.*

Tariq   Just tryin' to scare him.

Deema *grabs it off him.*

Deema   It's a notice of possession . . . we've got two weeks . . . He hasn't come out of his room for two days.

Tariq   So what's new?

Deema   He's gonna bury his head under the covers and hope it all goes away.

Tariq *is distressed and seems to be in pain.*

Tariq   I can't walk . . . feels like I'm dying . . . if I don't . . . if I don't get it . . . I . . . I'm gonna end up doin' something stupid . . . can't even sit down. Some dog tried to bite my arse.

Deema I can't take any more of all this shit . . . I just can't deal with it.

Tariq You should've seen it. Fuckin' great mangy thing . . . down by the railway bridge . . . was just walkin' past this 'ouse . . . I mean the front door . . . it was open and nobody was around . . . people round 'ere take silly chances, man . . . I walk up to it . . . tryin' to be a good neighbour . . . and this woman sets her Alsatian on me. He's going for me like he ain't eaten for days and she's flapping her arms up and down screamin' thieves like me should go back to their own country . . . I'm goin', I was born 'ere bitch . . . the cheek of it, Deem . . . she's the one who should have been locked up . . . I mean I could get rabies . . . I should get rabies . . . then I'd sue her arse.

Deema Shut up, Tariq. I had an interview . . . cabin crew . . . I could've bin seeing Rome, Paris . . . bloody Marrakech.

Tariq What interview?

Deema Don't matter.

She sits on the ground and **Tariq** *calms down, slowly making his way down to her clutching his leg as he does.*

Tariq C'mon, sis . . . that's wicked.

Deema He ain't gonna get the money.

Tariq You know Dad . . . last minute somethin'll turn up. You'll see . . . and you've got a job . . . that's good . . . you've gotta think about yerself. That's what I'm gonna do.

Deema I haven't got a job.

Tariq You just said, man.

Deema I had an interview.

Tariq You'll get it no probs.

Deema I di'n't go, alright.

Beat.

Tariq I'm gonna give this up . . . I'm gonna detox. I gotta be there with ya . . . start working. . .fed up with all this . . . you dunno how fed up I am.

Deema Jimmy came round for ya.

Tariq Fuck him.

Deema   He threatened me, Tariq . . .

Tariq   What's the arsehole said . . . I'll /

Deema   Wants the money you took.

Tariq   What you talking about?

Deema   Speaking a foreign language ain't I? You can't get out of this one. Said he's gonna sort you out. In Mum's house . . . you're gonna drag them into it . . . what the fuck are you doing?

Tariq   All mouth, man. Jimmy ain't even bin inside.

Deema   They don't need this . . . we've got other shit to do. I've got other shit to do, Tariq . . .

Tariq   I went to the clinic.

Deema   Just come see Mum or Dad, right.

Tariq   Listen to me. I waited ages to get an appointment.

Deema   That's good.

Tariq   I'm cutting down . . . by next week, I'll be almost clean I'm telling ya.

Beat.

I need . . . a last bit . . . just to cover the pain.

Deema *stands up chucking her cigarette away.*

Tariq   So can you help us?

Deema   With what?

Tariq   You heard what I said.

Deema   Ain't got nothing.

Tariq   Your wages.

Deema   My wages.

Tariq   Twenny quid that's all.

Deema   We have to get the phone reconnected.

Tariq *pulls out his girobook stuffed in the back of his jeans pocket and hands it to her.*

Beat.

It's due a week today. / You collect it and take your cut.

Deema   Next week.

Tariq   Please.

Beat.

You watch . . . it's all gonna change. Stop worrying and do your work. Can't keep takin' everythin' to heart.

Deema   You'll come home? Sort this out?

Tariq   Told you . . . I'll see Mum, talk to Dad . . . say hello an' that.

Beat.

Deema   Yeah?

Tariq   Yeah.

Deema *takes his hand and he pulls away.*

Tariq   I ain't a kid, man.

Beat.

Can I 'ave that score then?

First presented by Kali Theatre in October 2006 in a co-production with Birmingham Repertory Theatre and Soho Theatre.

Zameen

Satinder Chohan

Chandni Early twenties. Daughter of Baba, she is strong and independent-minded. She is wearing a brightly coloured shalwar kameez outfit with a sparkling chunni, juthis (traditional shoes) and gold accessories. Both Baba and Chandni are wearing a steel kara (Sikh bangle).

Baba Late fifties. A poor cotton-farmer. Widower and father of two children. His son Dhani is an alcoholic. Baba wears a traditional kurtha top and pyjama, a small orange turban and chappals on his feet.

Where India. A Punjabi village near Bathinda. The family room in a Punjabi pukka (brick and cement) house, painted a vibrant but paint-peeling shade of green. Doors, left and right, lead to the courtyard outside. A manja (charpoy) sits to the left and a peti (tin bridal trunk) sits to the right, draped in a hand-embroidered cotton white floral fabric. A jharu (small handheld broom) leans against the side of the trunk. On the back wall, a triptych of images hangs: a garlanded photograph of a chunni-clad older Sikh woman and painted portraits of a Sikh Guru and Punjabi revolutionary Bhagat Singh. Discarded tin containers labelled 'Bull Dose' in red, white and blue lettering dot the dusty floor. The family cotton field and a solitary Neem Tree can be seen on the horizon, through a window, bathed in an orange glow. Sound of crickets outside.

When Late monsoon season. Sunset.

What Has Just Happened The play focuses on Baba and his attempts to keep his land. A very good year's harvest has been followed by a very bad one and Baba is in deep debt to Lal, the rapacious local moneylender. Men dominate in this Jat community but Baba's daughter Chandni seeks to challenge the traditions.

The play begins with this scene. Baba and Chandni have just returned home from the wedding of a local village girl. They have entered the house in high spirits, dancing and singing and laughing together. They are now seated.

Baba (*blessing* **Chandni**'*s head*)   Shaavash. You're more than a perfect son, Chandni. You're a Lioness of Punjab too.

Chandni (*getting up*)   Does that mean that one day I'll roar over my own patch of land?

Baba   It means that now Preeto's married, I have to find a husband for you.

Baba *stretches his legs.* **Chandni** *walks over to the garlanded portrait.*

Chandni   Marigolds have faded so quickly. I only hung them up yester – (*Notices something on the garland.*) Ugh! What's . . . this . . .?

She removes the garland from the portrait and hurls it outside the door.

Are we all so busy we can't throw out a rotting garland?

Baba   Bheti, it's all anyone wanted to talk to me about at the wedding . . .

Chandni *grabs the broom and sweeps the floor.*

Chandni   What would you like for roti? I can make saag . . .

Baba   We should start looking soon . . .

Chandni   . . . or sabji or –

Baba   Bheti . . .?

Chandni (*hurling the broom aside*)   They wouldn't leave me alone either. Nothing better to do with their time than meddle.

Baba   What will the villagers say if we don't?

Chandni   Who cares what they say?

Baba   I have to.

Chandni   They should busy themselves marrying off their own children.

Baba   While I busy myself marrying off my own.

Chandni   She's barely been gone.

Baba   She would have wanted this, bheti.

Chandni   I'd rather look after the children at the school – than mother a husband and his family.

Baba   Lal once mentioned a travel agent in Jalandhar – one who helps our boys abroad. He might even find a way to get Dhani there . . .

Chandni   Acha? So Dhani goes abroad – and I live the rest of my life with a fat travel agent from Jalandhar? You're looking after your Lioness of Punjab so well.

Baba   Oh Raba, at least take a look . . .

Chandni   I don't want to follow up that moneylender's recommendations. Besides, you saw Preeto's dowry, all laid out on the veranda, like a sacred offering to her husband and in-laws. New television, new cupboard, new cooler, new table, new sofa set, new dish set, fridge, king-sized bed, queen-sized trunk, money and clothes – snaked in gold chains –

Baba   You forgot the motorcycle. So shiny and brand new! (*Drifts into a reverie.*) Oh to be riding across the plains of Punjab, tearing through dust storms, hot winds –

Chandni   A motorcycle without which Dhanwant's family threatened to cancel the wedding. Weddings don't celebrate husband and wife. They celebrate the wife's father's wallet. How will you pay for it all?

Baba   That's not your concern, bheti. Listen, my livelihood grows from the fragile stems of a single cotton crop. A simple thread ties me to the land – one that has the power to strangle me too. I've barely been breathing these past few years. But this year will be different. This year, the thread will unravel, run and run and run. Like those big, rich harvests of old. Soon, I'll be wealthy enough to send Dhani abroad – and throw you a lavish wedding at the best marriage palace on the GT Road.

Chandni *continues sweeping the floor.*

Baba   I was talking to Dhanwant earlier. He's started working for an Amrikan company investing in Punjab. They're looking into the cotton market here. Might even contract farm our cotton – at a competitive rate too.

Chandni   Sounds promising. But isn't his company building the new pipeline?

Baba   They're branching out into all sorts these days. Chardi kala, Punjab is ripe for picking! And very soon (*takes the broom from* **Chandni**, *helps her up and ties her chunni into a cotton sack*), I'll need you to sling a chunni sack on your back to cotton pick *our* riches.

Baba *admires* **Chandni** *in her cotton garb.*

Chandni   The crop is looking very full. Like her soft embroidered sheets, stretched out in the sun, bursting with flowers. Is it the seeds?

Baba   I bought so wisely this year, we'll be shifting cotton by the bale load! I'll even put cotton aside for you, to fill pillows and quilts for your dowry trunk.

Chandni *unties her cotton sack, throwing her chunni back around her neck.*

Baba   Then, straight after we harvest this crop, we'll comb the land quickly and sow a bumper wheat crop for Baisakhi. By which time, I'll also have found you a fine Jat boy.

Chandni (*sitting down*)   Doubt you'll need to look too long or too far.

Baba   You've someone in mind already? Hain?

Chandni *removes her gold accessories, laying them on the table.*

Chandni   There's hardly a lack of suitors in these villages. At the wedding, everywhere I turned, aunts, mothers, matchmakers were jostling to speak to me about this boy and that boy –

Baba   Hain, there was a demand. We could even compete with that rich girl – oh, what's her name? Dhanwant's boss's daughter . . .?

Chandni   Chhaya?

Baba   Hain, Chhaya.

Chandni   Her family could buy up all the single men round here if they wanted – and there are a few. You haven't noticed?

Baba   What?

Chandni   Our villages teeming with single boys?

Baba   Hain?

Chandni   There aren't enough girls for boys. Not enough wives to go round.

Baba   All this think talk is making you mad. How will we marry you off then?

Chandni   Baba, the villagers have spent years getting rid of their baby girls. Dumping their tiny skulls and bones on the roadside, in rivers, on rubbish heaps. Dissolving them in acid. Why? Because they're tiny kernels of nature. Not big kernels of profit. And only *now* these women are worried? Worried because there aren't enough brides for their sons and grandsons?

Baba   It's a terrible sin on us all, bheti. But the villagers are desperate. They're not wealthy.

Chandni   So better a small price to wash out a girl before birth than pay for her big dowry later?

Baba   The villagers still believe that with sons you invest, with daughters you're in debt. It's an expensive business raising a daughter and a dowry.

Chandni (*kneeling at* **Baba**'s *feet*)   What if I stayed here longer? Helped you work the land?

Baba   What's this twisted talk?

Chandni   Then I wouldn't need to get married. And we wouldn't need to raise a dowry.

Baba   Bheti, you can't grow old here. With the joy of seeing you grow into a woman is also the pain of knowing that one day soon I must let you go. You don't belong to me and you don't belong here. You belong to your husband and in-laws. Elsewhere.

Chandni (*standing*)   If I don't belong here, how is it that as your daughter, I'm entitled to half your land?

Baba   It's not your birthright.

Chandni   Yes, it is. By law.

Baba   Law? We don't live by the law when we live by tradition.

Chandni   What if I don't want to be like Preeto and the others, signing over my land to my brother?

Baba   There's barely enough to divide between sons nowadays. If our daughters sharpen their knives too, what will be left? A plot to feed the ants?

Chandni   There'll be nothing left when he's finished here.

Baba   I know you'll do what is right. If you don't want to, tell me now and I'll sign it all to him while I still can. Your land lies with your husband. This is Dhani's land.

Chandni   In my father's house, I own nothing. In my husband's house, I will own nothing. What do I own, Baba? Tell me, what can I call mine?

Baba   That's the way it is.

First presented by Kali Theatre in April 2008 at Manchester Contact, Leeds Playhouse, Arts Theatre, London, and on tour.

Gandhi and Coconuts

Bettina Gracias

Asha   Early thirties. Hindu. Lives with husband Ajay. They recently moved to London from Kerala, India so that Ajay could get a better job and send money home to the family. Asha spends most of her time alone in the flat, terrified to go out. She keeps the house spotless and enjoys cooking her husband's favourite dishes, all of which contain coconut, traditional in Keralan dishes. Asha loves her husband but is desperately lonely and imagines friends she doesn't have. She takes comfort in praying to the gods, especially Ganesh. Her life is routine; preparing breakfast for Ajay before he rushes out to work in the morning and preparing dinner in the evening, which he eats quickly before falling asleep in front of the TV.

Gandhi   Mohandas Karamchand Gandhi, born in India in 1869, was shot and assassinated in 1948. He was a freedom fighter who employed non-violent resistance to lead the successful campaign for India's independence from British rule.

Where   Asha and Ajay's open-plan, small flat. The walls are thin. The racist neighbour bangs and shouts abusively whenever Asha plays her music. Neighbours can also be heard complaining about the smell of **Asha**'s cooking which adds to her anxiety. In one corner is an altar decorated in fairy lights, with a statue of Ganesh.

When   Morning.

What Has Just Happened   The previous evening Asha decided that she would invite the neighbours to tea. Ajay has just left for work but Asha becomes too afraid to leave the flat so she holds an imaginary tea instead. Suddenly there is loud banging on the door; she is too scared to answer it and stays where she is. After a moment the doorbell rings. She sits completely motionless, not making a sound. It rings again, she holds her breath. The letterbox opens, Asha's eyes widen in fear. Gandhi's voice comes from outside.

Gandhi (*playfully*)   I know you're in there. Come on, open the door, Asha, I'm freezing out here.

Asha (*whispering*)   How do you know my name?

Gandhi   Asha! (*Beat.*) There's no point pretending, I know you're there.

She gets up cautiously and creeps to the door. She looks gingerly through the letterbox.

Ah, I can see you.

Asha   Who are you?

Gandhi   Open the door and you'll see.

Asha   Is this a trick?

Gandhi   What sort of trick could I be?

Asha   My neighbour.

Gandhi   He's not so good at accents.

Asha   Are you Indian?

Gandhi   It's freezing out here, I'm just wearing a loincloth.

Beat.

Come on. (*Teasing.*) Do you want the neighbours to see me?

Asha   Gandhi jee?

Gandhi   Who did you think I was? Nehru?

She stands there, aghast at the door.

Can I come in now?

Asha   But you're dead.

Gandhi   So what?

Asha   You're bleeding.

Gandhi   Of course I'm bleeding, I was shot.

Asha   But that was ages ago.

Gandhi   Blood doesn't stop.

Asha   You better come in.

Gandhi   Thank you.

She steps aside and lets him in. He enters, wearing only a loincloth with a blood-stained gunshot wound. He walks into the flat and stands grinning at **Asha** *happily.*

Gandhi   Thank you for your kind hospitality

He puts his hands together in the namaste greeting. **Asha** *does the same.*

Gandhi   (*looking around*)   You have a nice place.

Asha (*looks at his wound*)   Does it hurt?

Gandhi   Just a little irritating now and then, like some people, Nehru.

Asha   Would you like a plaster?

Gandhi *looks at her, stunned.*

Gandhi   Sixty-two years, and no one has offered me a simple plaster for my wounds. You are very kind.

Asha   If you're dead, why do you need a plaster?

Gandhi   I don't feel dead and it was your idea.

She touches him. He sinks happily into her touch and groans a little. She steps back.

Asha   How do I know you exist?

Gandhi   How do any of us know we exist? Touch me again, it feels so nice.

Asha   Don't play tricks with me, I know how tricky you are, were.

Gandhi (*happily*)   Do you?

Asha   That's not a compliment.

Gandhi   Oh.

Asha   You tricked the whole British army.

Gandhi (*pleased*)   I know.

Asha   And then you left a mess.

Gandhi   You know what I'd really like?

Asha   Sorry?

Gandhi   A nice cup of tea, with lots of sugar in it. I haven't had a cup of tea for sixty-two years.

Asha *looks at him strangely.*

Gandhi   What does it matter if I exist or not – will a simple cup of tea harm anyone?

Still looking at him suspiciously, **Asha** *gets up and goes into the kitchen area to put the kettle on. They watch each other.*

Gandhi   Do you have a biscuit?

Asha   I'm sorry, are you hungry?

Gandhi   Starving, ever since I died I feel unsatiated.

Asha   I have some jallebies.

Gandhi (*excited*)   Oh, I love jallebies.

Asha   Do you?

Gandhi   Particularly when they are hot and crispy on the outside, soft and syrupy on the inside, reminds me of something else.

He gives her a naughty smile.

Asha   Now I definitely know you're not real.

Gandhi   Because I like jallebies?

Asha   Yes.

Gandhi   That doesn't make sense.

Asha   Gandhi jee never indulged in any pleasures of the flesh, he was above such things.

Gandhi   I know, what a mistake, I regret it now.

Asha   Gandhi was pure.

Gandhi   Boring.

Asha   Strong.

Gandhi   Fanatical.

Asha   Single minded.

Gandhi   Dictatorial.

Asha   You are definitely not him.

Gandhi   Can we discuss this over some jallebies?

Asha   You're quite irritating.

Gandhi   Is this how you treat all your guests?

Asha   You're not my guest.

Gandhi   Some people would consider themselves honoured to have Gandhi in their living room.

Asha   Not when you're dead.

Gandhi   I was very sought after at the best dinner tables.

Asha   But you never ate anything.

Gandhi (*he sinks again*)   I know, I regret my fanaticism.

Asha   Everyone admired you.

Gandhi   I didn't need to go so far.

Asha   Maybe you did to achieve so much.

Gandhi *weighs this up with a nodding of his head.*

Gandhi   That's what I thought at the time. (*Beat.*) I thought I had to be a rod. That I could not waver. (*Beat.*) But now . . . I wonder.

Asha   We all make mistakes in life.

Gandhi   But we only get one.

Asha   Do we?

Gandhi *nods.*

Asha   There's no reincarnation?

Gandhi   Would I be here if there was?

Asha   Shame, I was looking forward to the next one.

Gandhi   That's my point, don't, don't look forward, enjoy it now, every moment, grab everything, seize it and hold it tight, eat as much as you can, eat everything, once it's gone, it's gone.

Asha   Either you're crazy or I am.

Gandhi   Or both.

She pokes his leg to see if he's real.

He grabs her hand and puts it on his leg, holding it there. She lets him.

He closes his eyes to savour her touch.

After a moment she grabs her hand away and stands up.

Asha   Get out of my head.

Gandhi *just smiles at her.*

Asha   Get out

Gandhi   Would you like me to leave?

Asha   Yes.

Gandhi *stands up.*

Gandhi   I was well brought up, it would be rude of me to stay.

Asha *walks to the door and holds it open.*

Asha   Good

Gandhi   I just thought you were lonely and you needed a little company. I didn't want to upset you, I'm sorry

Asha   Please leave.

Gandhi   May I make a suggestion?

Asha *just looks at him.*

Gandhi   Since you are feeling lonely.

Asha   I'm not lonely, I have a lovely husband.

Gandhi   Since you are *alone*, for now, why don't you just let me stay until your husband comes home – what harm can it do? Whether I exist or not? I am well-read and scintillating company . . . and . . . hungry.

He smiles charmingly at **Asha**.

Gandhi   I heard you were an excellent cook.

Asha   Did you?

Gandhi *nods.*

Gandhi   I love coconut.

Asha   But I only have chicken and you don't eat meat.

Gandhi   I do now. What harm can it do to entertain me for a few hours? (*Beat.*) We could have fun.

He gives her a charmingly cheeky look and smiles innocently at the same time.

Asha I did admire you.

He links arms with her and leads her unconsciously across the room into the kitchen area.

Gandhi Did you?

Asha I wish I was as brave.

Gandhi But you are, you came to this country, all alone.

Asha With Ajay.

Gandhi Without your family, or friends.

Asha But you were so brave, you fought for what you believed in. I'm too scared to do anything. I can't even leave the house.

Gandhi Were you like that in India?

Asha No, I wasn't afraid of anything.

Gandhi Maybe you should go back.

Asha That's not possible.

Gandhi Why not?

Asha Ajay has to work to support his family. He earns much more money than he could in India.

Gandhi What do you believe in?

Asha I'm a Hindu, like you.

Gandhi No, I mean, what do you, Asha, believe in, without all the teachings of the books, not what others tell you to believe.

Asha I don't know.

Gandhi *takes her hand in his gently.*

Gandhi Shall I tell you a secret?

Asha *nods.*

Gandhi Neither do I.

Asha But you were so strong and firm.

Gandhi On the outside. Inside I was shaking too.

Asha Really?

Gandhi   I followed the Bhagavad Gita to the letter – it was my rule book, my guide to life. I studied the truth in every verse but I never questioned the truth of the book, of the hand that wrote it.

Beat.

Now that I am dead, I have no guide book. I've been left alone, to think for myself, without rules.

She looks questioningly into his eyes and he looks back. There is a quiet moment of this.

You were dancing before I came

Asha   Yes.

Gandhi   Alone.

Asha   Yes.

Gandhi   Do you like to dance alone?

Asha   I'd rather dance with someone.

Gandhi   Your husband?

Asha   He won't anymore.

Gandhi   He used to?

Asha *nods.*

Gandhi   My wife loved to dance.

Asha   Did she?

Gandhi   But I never danced with her.

Asha   You were too busy.

He stands up and bows to **Asha**.

Gandhi   Dance with me now.

Asha *looks around embarrassed.*

Gandhi   There's no one to see

Asha *giggles.*

Asha   Ok.

He takes her arms and leads her into a waltz, trying to guide her but she does not know it.

Gandhi   You dance nicely.

Asha   I've never danced like this . . . touching . . .

Gandhi   I learned in England. It was the one thing I admired about the British, the way they danced, so light and graceful, like they were dancing on air.

Asha *suddenly looks at the clock and realises the time. The music stops.*

Asha   You have to go

She heads for the door and holds it open.

Gandhi (*smiling*)   We had fun.

Asha   Please.

Gandhi   Tell me we had fun.

Asha   We had fun.

Gandhi   We could have more.

Asha *shakes her head.*

Gandhi   If I don't exist, he won't see me.

Asha   Please go, quick.

Gandhi   Wouldn't you like to know?

Asha *shakes her head. He bows in namaste.*

First presented by Kali Theatre in November 2010 at Arcola Theatre, and in January 2011 on tour to Plymouth Drum, Leicester Curve and The Public, West Bromwich.

Behna

Sonia Likhari

Dal (Daljit) Thirty. British Punjabi, from Southall, London. As the eldest of three sisters, in a family that would have preferred to have boys, she has been the 'sensible and reliable' daughter. Dal has been suffering from depression and low self-esteem. She's a comfort eater and has struggled with her weight since she was a child. Unhappily married to Jag, they have two young children, a daughter and son.

Simi (Simran) Late twenties. Dal's younger sister. Simi is British Punjabi from Southall, London and has a Southall accent. Married to Sunny. She is naturally confident but through the duration of the play she undergoes a transformation (having IVF treatment to conceive the child she longs for) and skin grafts after an accident at the end of Act One, where half of her face is seriously burnt with hot oil.

Where London, Southall. A Sikh household kitchen in a terraced house, a few nights before the wedding of the youngest daughter, Tina.

When Evening.

What Has Just Happened It's ladies' sangeet night and the general hubbub and singing of traditional wedding songs can be heard softly offstage. Dal is alone in the kitchen looking hot and frazzled, frying samosas. She's kept a couple aside and is eating as she goes. She checks the time and looks impatiently out of the window. She's wearing a plain, everyday salwaar kameez. Simi enters in high spirits. By contrast to Dal, she is dressed in the latest Bollywood fashion. This scene is at the beginning of the play.

NB: To sustain this as a duologue, the extract has been edited to remove additional entrances and exits by other characters and this is denoted by ***

Simi Hi, Dal, you alright? Sorry / I'm late

Dal Bout bloody time you turned up /

Simi I know, I know, sorry. We got held up in traffic /

Dal   Knew you'd say that /

Simi   No we did seriously /

Dal   Yeah yeah.

Simi   Don't believe me then.

Dal   D'you know how long I've been in here slaving my bloody guts out? How come I can get here on time? It's not by magic you know.

Simi   Alright! I'm sorry. Seen the back room? It's heaving. It's like wall-to-wall women

Dal   I do know. I've been cooking for them.

Simi   Took me ages to get through, people kept calling me over /

Dal   Didn't stop for a chat then.

Simi   No! Mum sent me straight in here . . . I was gonna do that anyway . . .

Dal   Yeah right.

Simi   I was! (*Beat.*) Why isn't anyone else helping?

Dal   Mum was going on and on about her bloody corns so I sent her packing.

Simi   You didn't fall for that? She can stand and gossip for hours in the gurdwara kitchen.

Dal   Yeah, well . . . I thought she should be out there anyway, you know, with Tina . . . doing mother of the bride stuff . . .

Simi   Yeah and Tina's looking well pissed-off with her! She's having her mehndi put on so she can't even escape. And there's Mum fussing around telling the beautician how to do her job.

Dal   She's not is she?

Simi   Can you believe it? Mum giving beauty tips? A woman who still rubs lipstick on her cheeks. Remember when she used to have those two coins of red /

Dal/Simi   Like Coco the Clown!

Dal   Oh God don't remind me! (*Beat.*) You look nice

Simi   Thanks! Have I seen this suit before?

Dal   Probably. I didn't see the point in dressing up. Bet you spent hours getting ready, you always do. Dunno how Sunny puts up with you

Simi   He's well compensated.

Beat.

Dal   That's the last of the samosay, thank God. My feet are killing me and there's still all the bloody pathooray to make.

Simi   You are joking – we'll be stuck in here ages missing all the fun /

Dal   Hoping all the work would be finished if you got here late enough, were you?

Simi   No.

Dal   Hoping good old Dal would have it sorted, like she always does? After all, Dal likes being in the kitchen, doesn't she, she enjoys cooking, the more mouths to feed the better. God you're selfish!

Simi   Oh, right, of course, yeah, I'm so selfish. That's why I've come straight in here to help /

Dal   Help? You haven't even started and you're already moaning. I can see how much you're expecting to help, all dolled up like flippin' Ashwaria Rai.

Simi   Just because you're wearing some old . . . No. I'm not doing this. Let's just get everything finished in here so we can at least enjoy some of the night. Tell me what you want me to do.

Dal   Here, you can gun the atta (knead the dough).

Simi *takes the bowl of dough from* **Dal** *and looks at it distastefully. Touches the dough gingerly and makes half-hearted efforts to knead it.* **Dal** *gets on with rearranging the samosay on the plate.*

Simi   So, do you really reckon I look like Ashwaria Rai? Cos Sunny always says I look like Praveen Babi. But she's dead isn't she, so /

Dal   What are you doing with that atta?

Simi   It's going to get right under my new nails. Let me do something else instead.

Dal   God's sake. Hand these samosas round then. Make sure you come straight back, alright? I'm not doing all this on my own.

Simi *hands over the bowl and takes the plate of samosas instead. Exits.*

***

Dal *continues kneading the dough. She stuffs a big bite of samosa into her mouth.* **Simi** *enters and* **Dal** *turns away wiping her mouth surreptitiously.*

Simi   I can't believe this. We're missing everything! All because you wouldn't back me up. I wanted to get caterers in but you were like, 'Oh no, that'll be far too expensive. We can manage the cooking ourselves.'

Dal   Mum and Dad can't afford it, you know that, Simi. I didn't notice you offering to foot the bill for caterers.

Simi   Whatever. (*Food smells draw her to the cooker.*) Mmm . . . boneless chicken. Your speciality. (*Has a taste.*) Mmm yum! What else is there?

Dal   Aloo gobi and kaalay cholay.

Simi   Sunny loves kaalay cholay. Bloody restaurants don't do it. We have to go round his mum's whenever he gets the taste for it.

Dal   Useless you are.

Simi   Can't all be Mrs Perfect Housewife you know.

Dal   Can't be bothered you mean.

Simi   Well . . . yeah alright!

From offstage sound of Mum singing traditional wedding song.

That's Mum! She's doing gidha! (wedding dance).

Dal   Oh God, they better give her lots of room.

Simi   I can't see!

Hubbub is louder as **Simi** *tries to watch the action. She gives up and starts her own 'gidha' instead, clapping, dancing, singing and coaxing* **Dal** *who eventually joins in.*

Simi   Can you believe she's actually getting married! Our Tina Tomboy.

Dal   I know.

Simi   I had to bully her into wearing a bra and now look at her. More into fashion than I am! I've got to be here really early on Saturday morning to do her make-up.

Dal   I thought that mehndi woman's doing it

Simi No way! I'm not about to let some bhindu make-up artist near my little sister. They always use really dark plummy colours and Tina's way too gori (white) for that, just like me . . . well, us really I suppose. Did she show you her wedding lengha? We found it in Damini's and oh my God, Dal, it is so beautiful. It's this really lovely tangerine colour? No boring reds or pinks, that's so old fashioned. The colour really sets off her complexion you know and the dupatta's got loads of gold in it. She's going to look just like a ray of sunshine walking into the gurdwara /

Dal God's sake Simi.

Simi What, it's exciting! I can't wait to see her all done up. (*Beat.*) Your Jag's looking pretty good isn't he, in his fancy new gear? He looks like he's lost a bit of weight. (*Beat.*) How's your diet going?

Dal Who said I'm on a diet?

Simi I thought you were.

Dal Well, I'm not.

Simi So what are you going to wear on Saturday?

Dal I was thinking, maybe, clothes?

Simi I'm only asking /

Dal Oh yeah, really subtle aren't you? How's the diet going? Your husband looks fit.

What are you going to wear?

Simi Bit touchy

Dal You're so full of it. Princess Simran. You probably put on your best chania choli before you clean the toilet!

Simi At least I've got standards.

Dal Least I've got standards. You'll never see me without my make-up. I even re-apply it before I go to bed. Pathetic.

Simi Oh I'm pathetic. You're a flipping disgrace /

Dal Am I /

Simi We've got all the relatives out there, people filming for the wedding video and you look like a sack of potatoes! If you can't respect yourself you could at least think about the family's respect.

Dal   Don't you talk to me about respect. If it wasn't for me them lot would have all died of hunger by now. I keep this bloody family together. I'm the eldest, and nobody ever lets me forget it do they? It's me who has to keep everything locked up inside me just to maintain this family's respect.

Simi   What do you mean?

Dal   Forget it.

Simi   No, come on, I want to know. I don't need anyone covering up for me, so if this has got anything to do with my smoking, let's just go and tell Mum and Dad now.

Dal   Smoking /

Simi   You've been holding that over me for years. It's old news, Dal. No one bloody cares, not once you're married.

Dal   I couldn't give a toss about you smoking.

Simi   So what is this great big burden you're carrying to protect us all.

Silence. **Dal** *making balls out of dough ready to roll out.*

Simi   Surprise, surprise. Nothing to say /

Dal   This isn't the time.

Simi   Yeah, very convenient excuse.

First presented by Kali Theatre in March 2010, in real kitchens in houses in Birmingham and the Black Country.

Endless Light

Sayan Kent

Nadia Mid-thirties. Glamorous and extremely rich, displaying her wealth in her expensive Western clothes and jewellery. She is from Kolkata, West Bengal, and is of dual heritage (Indian father, English mother). Nadia inherited land from her father, which she is now mining for coal. She is single.

Red Late twenties. Working class. An actor from London – he is charismatic, charming and self-serving.

Where India, Kolkata. Nadia's plush office overlooking the city.

When Evening.

What Has Just Happened The play is set in the present/near future in Kolkata, south of which is the sacred (fictional) Vardasi mountain, once covered in trees but now a quarry.

Chandra is Nadia's estranged sister (the sisters were brought up separately in the UK and India respectively following their parents' divorce). Chandra is an environmental activist and the previous evening flew to the Vardasi mountain by helicopter with two fellow activists to globally publicise the detrimental effects of the mining. Nadia and Chandra unexpectedly met there, the event provoking considerable hostility between them as they voiced their differing attitudes to the mountain and Nadia's mining activities.

Red has come to India to try and reignite his relationship with Chandra (who is his former lover) but so far to no avail. Red met Nadia for the first time at a charity gala function. This is their second meeting and they have just returned to her office from a similar event. He does not know that Nadia is Chandra's sister and Nadia holds this back from him. It is late. They have been drinking. There is chemistry between them.

Nadia *picks up a bottle of champagne, which she is slowly opening.*

Nadia   They all blur into one big synchronised swim of jaws going up and down yah-yah-yah meaningless words flowing out flooding the air with lung vapour and spit I hate sycophants.

You do drink this? Of course you do, it's expensive.

Red   Got any beer?

Nadia   No.

Red   I've had to drink that shit all night.

Nadia *laughs loudly. He loosens his tie and undoes his top shirt button.*

Nadia   How are you finding the weather? It's just like England now, rain all seasons.

Red   I don't bother moaning about the weather anymore. The fun's gone out of it now the whole world goes on about it. Wet, dry, too hot here, too cold there, farty typhoons somewhere else blowing the junks to Timbuktu.

She opens the bottle and pours out two glasses.

Nadia   So here we are again? I might think you were following me.

Red   Or are you following me?

Nadia   Possibly. Mishka's cast you in his film? He's very taken with you.

Red   He's gay.

Nadia   So?

Red   He keeps asking me to dinner.

Nadia   Go, his dinners are legendary.

Red   What for? Being buggered after the cheese course.

She hands him a glass.

Nadia   He doesn't serve cheese.

Red *raises his glass.*

Red   Bottoms up.

They drink.

Why do you pay good money for this stuff?

Nadia   I don't, it's given to me. When you're rich people give you things all the time so you stay rich.

Red   When you're poor you get fuck-all.

Nadia   Tragic, isn't it? Did you find the woman you came here for?

He looks at her then, slightly on guard, chooses to ignore the question and looks out at the lights of the night-time cityscape.

Red   What we going to do when all the lights go out?

Nadia   The environmentalist. Chandra, wasn't it?

Red   Does it frighten you? The darkness. Knowing it's coming.

Nadia   I don't dwell on it.

Red   She thinks it can be stopped –

Nadia   So you have seen her.

Red   If the international community –

Nadia   Do you love her? –

Red   put pressure on – governments – shit.

Nadia   What?

Red   I came all this way.

Nadia   Nobody's ever done that for me.

Red   All this way – I thought I knew her but I was wrong.

Nadia   My father looked on me with derision whenever I was wrong.

Red   You never really know people.

Nadia   All I ever wanted was his approval.

Red   I'm just going to have a good time.

Nadia   Did your father approve of you?

Red (*quietly and close up to her*)   My father was a cunt.

Nadia   Ask Chandra to meet me.

Red   Ask her yourself.

A smile creeps over her face.

Nadia   I want you to.

Red   I don't want to.

Pause.

Nadia   Why does she call you Red?

Red   It's my name.

Nadia   Your name's Adam. Why does she call you Red?

Red   Because I like tomatoes.

Nadia   We all have something we keep locked away in our hearts.

She laughs slightly but unconvincingly.

Red   Where's the slug?

Nadia   Slug?

Red   He who never takes his eyes off you. Trails behind. Beady antennae – watching.

Nadia   Mohan? (*Laughs.*)

Red   He's probably under a table somewhere or in a cupboard making sure I don't make any sudden moves on you.

Nadia   Oh, that's exciting.

Red   Ready to slide out and stun me with slime.

Nadia   Mohan is a very loyal slug.

Red   So loyal he keeps other men away from you.

Nadia   You're here.

Red   Does he turn you on?

Nadia   Mohan?

Red   His eyes linger on you a little too –

Nadia   When?

Red   People think he's your shag.

Nadia *laughs.*

Nadia   He repulses me

Red   He controls you, and you like it.

Nadia   Are you jealous?

Beat.

Red   I'm not interested in you.

He walks away from her.

Nadia (*cooler*)   Why did you come back with me?

Red   I was bored.

Nadia   If you ask nicely, I'll show you around.

She begins to undress.

Red   The slug wouldn't allow it.

Nadia   That's true.

Red   Is he watching us now?

Nadia   He doesn't spy on me.

Red   Do you have any privacy?

Nadia   Privacy isn't so much about who knows, but who tells.

She pulls at his clothes, undressing him.

Red   Did you raise a ton of money for Unicef?

Nadia   You have a caring side –

Red   I like kids.

Nadia   The sycophants pay whatever's asked, they like to be seen as generous.

How generous were you?

Red   I'm not a sycophant.

Nadia   Oh no, I forgot. What are you?

Red   I'm still paying off my debts.

Nadia   You want money? You only have to ask.

Red   Money makes slaves of people.

Nadia   Love makes slaves of people, Red.

He lies back on the desk. She climbs on him.

First presented by Kali Theatre in January 2012 at Southwark Playhouse as part of a double bill with *Purnjanam/Born Again* by Sharmila Chauhan.

Mustafa

Naylah Ahmed

Mustafa Late thirties. Practising Muslim. Mustafa is wearing a thaveez around his neck on a black cord. Both Mustafa and his brother Shabir came to England as children. They do not have Asian accents. Mustafa's pronunciation will be correct in both Arabic and Urdu for someone with Pakistani heritage. He's not as posh as his brother.

Shabir Early forties. Mustafa's older brother. Not religious. Married. Drinks. Shabir is a well-spoken, successful solicitor. He pronounces Urdu/Islamic words in an Anglicised way. He has just been promoted to a partner in his firm. Smartly dressed.

Where UK prison. A room for prisoner meetings with their legal representatives – known amongst the prison staff as the goldfish bowl as it has a large glass window for officers outside to keep an eye. A table and two chairs sit in the middle of the room.

When Present day. Afternoon.

What Has Just Happened Mustafa has been imprisoned for the death of a young man during an 'exorcism'. He is awaiting trial, charged with manslaughter. During his time in prison he has alienated both inmates and staff alike with strange supernatural incidents frequently occurring in his presence with the most recent just the previous night. Mustafa's older brother Shabir lost touch when Shabir left home. The exorcism victim's father has asked Shabir to represent Mustafa and appeal against his sentence. Shabir is returning to try and make amends and get started on preparing the brief, after their first prison meeting ended badly. He does not have a tie on today, his collar is undone and his jacket is over his arm when he enters the room. He puts his jacket and case down and remains standing.

Shabir Okay, so we got off on the wrong foot the other day. I'm sorry if it was anything I said. I appreciate it can't be easy in here . . . it must be . . . Anyway, I'm sorry it's taken longer than I said to come back. (*Beat.*) Mustafa?

Mustafa How's your wife?

Shabir   She's . . . good, she's fine, thanks, thanks for asking . . .

Look, this is all nice, you and me and this. But bottom line, it isn't going to help us get you out of here.

Mustafa   I don't think they let murderers go that easily, Shabir.

Shabir   Manslaughter. You've been convicted and sentenced for manslaughter with diminished responsibility. Unless you're telling me something new?

Mustafa   A boy died. Whatever they call it whatever terms you use . . .

Shabir   These aren't 'terms'. Mustafa it's the law. Manslaughter with diminished responsibility – fourteen years – do you know what that means?

You look worse than last time. Have you slept?

Mustafa   No. Had a . . . visitor.

Shabir   Who? Malik?

Mustafa   No. Forget it. Look I never intended to get you mixed up in this.

Shabir   Well, that's the thing about family isn't it; intend it, don't intend it, it makes no difference.

Mustafa   Why are you here?

Shabir   What? I told you, Malik asked me –

Mustafa   I mean why did you come. When you found out?

Shabir   Isn't it obvious?

Mustafa   They giving you a hard time at work?

Shabir   Look we need to –

Mustafa   Are they?

Shabir   I'm a partner. While you were away I . . . I'm a partner at the firm now.

Mustafa   Congratulations.

Shabir   One with a brother who's been convicted of killing some kid during an exorcism. Congratulations are . . . pointless.

Mustafa   That's why you're here.

Shabir   What difference does it make?

Mustafa   A lot. To me.

Shabir   Wish you'd have stayed in Pakistan. Mind you I don't know what you were up to over there.

Mustafa   Training, I guess.

Shabir   Oh for heaven's sake – you weren't . . . Please don't tell me you were up some mountain with a Kalashnikov!

Mustafa   Ibaadat – I was learning under Aamil Zahid Hus(sain) –

Shabir   Oh that would be right. I should have known, minute you hit the ground I bet you were off in some cave meditating with nothing but your thasbee and a –

Mustafa   Don't do this.

Shabir   Why? A boy is dead, just like you said.

Mustafa   Yes.

Shabir   There are people out there who are mourning your sentence, thinking you *saved* this boy from some . . . some . . .

Mustafa   Djinn. You can't even say it . . . And what do the others think? Some people think I'm a hero and the others . . .?

Shabir   Think you're a crazed mullah who killed a boy who may have suffered from a mental disorder.

Mustafa *gets up and kicks back his chair.* **Shabir** *nods through the glass to an officer indicating everything is okay.*

Mustafa   If you think that then you really shouldn't be (here) –

Shabir   That's not what I said.

Mustafa   But it's what you're thinking.

Shabir   Is it?

Mustafa (*pointing*)   There.

Shabir (*looking down at his body*)   What?

Mustafa   That vein on your neck. It's twitching. Always twitches when you're nervous.

Shabir   I'm not nerv(ous) –

Mustafa   Yeah you are. You're trying to convince me to appeal when you don't believe I should.

Shabir   What I am doing is acting as your legal representative.

Mustafa   How much did you have to drink before you came here?

Shabir   What?

Mustafa   How much – surely as your client I deserve to know?

Beat.

Don't look now, but it's twitching.

Shabir   Fuck you.

Mustafa   Here's the thing, Shabir. Some people think I'm a hero and some people think I'm a murderer. But they're all out there living their lives and I'm in here. Alone. And there's nothing you can do about it.

Shabir   I can get a sentence reduction. I know I can.

He grabs his bag and empties some files onto the table.

Tell me what happened.

Mustafa   You've read the files.

Shabir   I want to know from you, first.

Mustafa   I can't do this . . .

Shabir   Everything. Start with the boy.

*He looks at **Mustafa**. This is it, make or break. They both look out at the officer. **Shabir** gestures for **Mustafa** to sit. He does so. This isn't going to be easy for him, but he sits.*

Mustafa   He wasn't just some kid. You know him. Kamran. I taught him Qur'an from maybe four, five years old.

Shabir   I remember.

Mustafa   He wanted to be a hafiz but his mom wasn't up for it.

Shabir   Because of you?

Mustafa   Because it meant his secular education would take a backseat and she didn't want that. Didn't want the Qur'an to take up space in his mind that GCSE biology might need . . . I stopped teaching him when he was about eight, he was a quick learner, finished the Qur'an about three times while he was with me. But I still saw him around after that, saw his dad.

Shabir Malik.

Mustafa Yeah. Lived close by for years, saw them all the time . . .

Shabir So when this . . . happened he was seventeen?

Mustafa Yes. I went to Pakistan. I got back, over a year ago now. Didn't see Malik or Kamran. Heard people talking about them though, saying the boy had lost weight, lost his hair . . . They said he was possessed.

Shabir So you went to see him?

Mustafa No. I prayed for him. Then one day Malik comes to my door. He was in a state. He wanted me to come and see his son – he'd only just heard I was back.

Shabir And . . .?

Mustafa He wasn't the boy I remembered. Was older, of course, but smaller – least it seemed like it. Weak, thin, pulled half his hair out – bitten the inside of his cheeks out . . .

Shabir Had they been to a doctor?

Mustafa Didn't ask.

Shabir But –

Mustafa I'm not a physician – that's not why I was there. He'd been like that for over a year apparently. Whole family was . . . sad, burdened. House was black with smoke in places. They hadn't bothered to fix it, paint it.

Shabir Smoke?

Mustafa Malik said if they upset him – if he got angry – fires would just start up. Kitchen, corner of the living room – telly exploded.

Shabir So you agreed to an exorcism?

Mustafa No. I saw the boy, sat with him. We prayed together. Seemed to be doing okay, even ate with him, to encourage him, and he managed to get some food in and some sleep. Then one day I'm sitting on the settee with Malik and his daughter and Kamran gets angry. Starts yelling, kicking off.

Shabir Kicking off?

Mustafa   Screaming, he was in a rage – his voice wasn't his own it was . . .

Shabir   There are mental conditions that –

Mustafa   He grabbed one foot of the settee and lifts it right up – with us three still on it. Three, maybe four feet in the air. Slams it down. His sister goes flying, Malik starts having an asthma attack . . .

Shabir *scribbles a note down.*

Mustafa   Mental conditions exist, course they do, voices can change, people self-harm . . . But no one lights a fire in a room they're not in without so much as a match . . . no one lifts three people and a settee four foot into the air one-handed cos of some mental disorder.

Shabir   But with all the chaos and Malik's asthma – the family were already so distressed that . . .

Mustafa   They imagined it? That we all hallucinated together?

Shabir   I'm not (saying that) –

Mustafa   Yes you are. I don't know what it is about the truth when it gets a bit difficult, out of the norm. Passes from me to you and it becomes . . . a tale. A comic book bit of entertainment.

Shabir   I'm trying to understand.

Mustafa   So if you don't understand then it's not true? It didn't happen?

Shabir   This is no time for philosophising Mustafa. You went into a room with a perfectly healthy seventeen-year-old and when you came out he was dead.

Mustafa   Perfectly healthy? Have you been listening to anything I've –

Shabir   He was alive. He was alive and then he wasn't. You were in there with him. You were the only one in there with him.

Mustafa   You're trying to make sense out of it. Cold, British, legal sense. Your face looks just like the barrister and the jury and the judge. You should go.

Shabir   Mustafa –

Mustafa   It's time for Asr.

Shabir   See, this is what you do – always – you walk away.

Mustafa   I'm not going anywhere. Not for a long time.

Shabir   And I want to change that. But I just don't see how –

Mustafa   You don't have to see, you have to believe.

Shabir   You pleaded not guilty.

Mustafa   Yes.

Shabir   How can you refuse an appeal – accept their punishment – when you pleaded not guilty?

Mustafa   I'm in prison because a boy died. I pleaded not guilty because I didn't take his life. But he died, and I can't change that.

He stands. **Shabir** *begins, reluctantly, to gather his things together.*

First presented by Kali Theatre in March 2012 at Soho Theatre and on tour in a co-production with Birmingham Repertory Theatre and Soho Theatre.

The Husbands

Sharmila Chauhan

Aya   Mid-thirties, Indian. Aya is happily married with two husbands,
Sem and Omar. As the political leader of Shaktipur, Aya is radical
and visionary wanting to take the principles of her community beyond
its current reach and help women throughout India. Her imminent
marriage to a man from Mumbai is her first step in enabling this
expansion to take place. Aya is concealing the fact that she is in the
early stages of pregnancy as this would not allow her to take a third
husband.

Omar   Mid- to late thirties. Male. Omar was born by the coast, outside
Shaktipur. When he married Aya, he moved to Shaktipur and brought his
mother with him. Sensual and strong willed, he has an easy, self-assured
manner, but is quick tempered. He wants Aya to have a baby and settle
down and stop working so much.

Where   India, Shaktipur. The kitchen of the family home.

When   Late morning. The day of Aya's third marriage.

What Has Just Happened   Shaktipur is a large community of about
5,000 people in Kerala, southern India. Set in the future, this rural
community was set up as a response to diminishing numbers of girls in
India as a consequence of increasing levels of female feticide and
infanticide. Here women practise polyandry, marrying several times.
Aya's two other husbands have a warm brotherly relationship, but Omar
is worried that the arrival of a third husband will unbalance the harmony
and divert Aya's affections away from him, destroying what they have
together. Omar enters carrying dirty bed sheets and personal items from
Aya's bedroom. Aya is sitting on the floor preparing flowers for a
garland.

Aya   Why are you doing that?

Omar   Why not?

Aya   It is not your job.

Omar   I need these things.

Aya   Come sit.

She pats the space next to her.

Omar   I want to take these to *my* room.

He drops the sheets on the floor. On top lie some of his personal effects – a book, some clothing. He sits down. She rubs his back.

Aya   You can leave your belongings in my room.

Omar   I prefer to take them

Aya   As you wish. But you will find them back there soon enough.

Omar   You will need space for your new husband will you not?

Aya   I did not ask you to move them.

Beat.

Omar   Perhaps I will take them to the coast.

Aya   When?

Omar (*a little afraid*)   When I next go.

Aya *returns to her task. Refusing to react to* **Omar***'s threat.*

Aya   You know garland making is the job of the husbands.

Omar   Then let me.

Aya   No. I'll do it.

For you . . .

Aya *continues with the garlands.*

Aya   I want them to be heavy.

Omar   You have enough.

Aya *finds one last flower.*

Omar   The thread will break.

Aya *threads it on.*

Aya   Are you so sure?

Omar   Maybe not now.

But at the ceremony.

Aya *adds the last one, smiling at* **Omar**. *Cajoling him almost to disagree. The garland is complete.*

Aya A garland should be like a chain of gold

Looking light

But feels heavy.

She fingers **Omar**'*s chain.*

Aya I thought this one would suit you best.

Omar I thought it was Mother who chose them.

Aya It should have been Mother.

But I told her

If I have to see them everyday, then

Surely it is for me to choose.

Omar Like your husbands?

. . .

Like your *new* husband?

Aya *laughs.*

Aya Come, my love.

She stands and takes the sacred bottle from her pocket and dabs the blood on his neck. As she does so, he takes a kiss from her. She does not object, but does not fully engage either.

Omar You feel I always want too much, but I wish simply to feel your heart.

Aya (*laughing*) My heart?

Omar Last night as you lay there, coated in the sweat of pleasure,

You turned your back on me.

Aya (*surprised*) What does that mean, Omar?

If I turn toward or away from you –

After the fact?

That I love you less?

Omar   You never used to do that.

Aya (*weary*)   I was tired.

Omar   You were *tired*?

Aya   Well, yes . . .

Pleasure is exhausting sometimes.

Omar   So now you complain of that also?

Aya   I do not complain.

I state fact . . .

I was tired.

Omar   So you turned away?

Aya   So I went to sleep.

Omar   And today?

Aya   Today I am not tired

Yet.

Omar   And tonight you bring someone else to your bed.

Aya   This is *the way*.

Omar   This wasn't *our* way.

Aya   This is the way.

The way it's always been . . .

You've always known that.

Omar (*shaking head, voice low*)   No . . .!

I knew you were a grieving widow.

Your first husband dead.

His brother in a separate bed!

Aya *reaches out to him and caresses him.*

Omar   You have energy for everything.

Shaktipur, the land, even trips to the city

But not us

Not anymore . . .

Aya (*frustrated*)   This again?!

Omar   When we make love you close your eyes.

It's as if your mind is somewhere else

Rummaging through old memories, or finding new possibilities

Anywhere but with me.

Aya   We are together as often as we used to . . .

Omar   Your body is there, but your heart is not, Aya . . .

You do not talk to me as you used to . . .

Why is it always up to me to entice you?

Do you think it's only this (*touching her*) that I want?

That I don't *feel* anything?

Aya   Of course I don't

But you're always demanding something, Omar . . .

Always wanting more . . .

Omar   And why shouldn't I? You're my wife!

Aya   Why do you say that?

'Your wife', your belonging . . .

Omar   How could you understand, Aya?

I am but one star in the sky to you

But to me, you are the silver moon.

Aya *smiles, sad.*

Omar   You've closed yourself to me.

I can feel it . . .

Aya *creates physical distance between them. Upset.*

Omar (*quiet, almost to self*)   You think I can't do it

That I am cold and infertile

But I am not, Aya. *I am not.*

Aya *is not able to look at him.*

Aya (*whispering*)   I know.

Beat.

But what can I do?

Omar (*shaking his head*)   I can not . . .

Can not Aya.

Aya   You can!

We can endure this

You/we have to.

Aya *wraps her arms around his shoulders.*

Aya   Remember when your mother found us in the boat that night?

Omar   Of course.

Aya   She said that she didn't know how an old woman like me could move like that!

Omar   You *liked* to make it rock . . .

Aya (*smiling*)   Maybe . . .

Omar   Remember the water used to come in and soak the bottom?

You didn't care . . .

Aya   I did. Just not as much as you

Omar   The noise used to wake the neighbours . . .

Aya   It was embarrassing

Sometimes.

Beat.

Omar   And now you want me to listen to you and him?

He turns to face her, pushing her hands away.

I do not know what you want of me, Aya.

Am I your friend, your lover, your confidant?

Aya (*sighing*)   I told you once

Love is a meal.

You can not have one dish without the other.

Omar   You'll never understand . . .

Aya   I understand you loved your boat.

Loved it as much as your mother hated me.

Omar   Is that why you asked me to give it all up?

My life outside this place?

My freedom?

Aya (*slightly defiant*)   Yes.

Omar (*quietly flattered*)   She doesn't hate you.

She's a mother.

She wants grandchildren . . .

Aya   Like all mothers.

Once is not enough

They want everyone to do it!

Beat.

Omar   Does he make you happy, Aya?

Happier than me?

Aya (*genuine*)   No.

I still love you the same.

Omar   But you still bring him

To give you a child?

Beat.

(*Frustrated.*) To give you what I can not!

Aya   No, no.

For the community

For all of this!

(*Softer, coming closer to him.*) I want you . . .

She *tries to kiss him.* **Omar** *resists.*

Omar   Don't touch me . . .

Aya   I don't want this to change us

Change the way you make me feel alive

Feel free . . .

Omar   So free you can . . . /

Aya   Shhhh . . . I want to protect this as much as you.

Beat.

Believe me, when I say

It is not about a child.

Can you understand there are parts of a room that remain undiscovered?

Omar   And me? Do you think you know me so well?

Aya   I know it is not fair . . . But I try my best to let you have your freedoms.

Omar   But I do not want those freedoms, Aya!

Aya   Perhaps not now but /

Beat.

We will be together always.

Omar *lets her take his hand.*

Aya   My love, whether there is another husband or not

I promise you, *if* I have a child it will be yours.

Omar   And the others?

Aya   I promise:

It will be yours.

He grasps her hand tighter. **Aya** *caresses him, but physically seeking reassurance at the same time, perhaps wrapping* **Omar**'s *arms around her.*

Omar   You mean that? This is not just about the bedroom, Aya.

*They kiss, long and hard. **Aya** laughs.*

Aya No, not about just the bedroom.

Omar *pushes **Aya** down and unwraps her clothes.*

Omar Shhh.

Aya I surrender.

Omar I didn't ask you to.

Aya No?

She undresses him.

Then, just a taste. A small taste.

He resists a little.

Omar You can never have just a taste, my love.

Aya You will always be here.

She touches her heart. He smiles.

She unwraps her sari. He sits her down in front of him and plays a finger up and down her spine. She sighs in pleasure.

Aya I still need you . . .

Omar *holds her close, clearly aroused.*

Aya (*softer*) Want you . . .

Omar *moves his hands to her lower back and then begins kissing her neck.*

Aya We will go *together*

To your boat

Make it move again.

First presented by Kali Theatre in February 2014 at Plymouth Drum, Soho Theatre and on tour in a co-production with Pentabus Theatre.

The Dishonoured

Aamina Ahmad

Shaida Aged seventeen. Pakistani. A prostitute. Shaida is a young woman who does everything with a seriousness beyond her years. In her private moments she enjoys reading Urdu poetry and has a book by Faiz on the bedside table.

Colonel Tariq Aged thirty-eight. Pakistani. Middle class. A highly decorated army officer working for the ISI (Pakistan Intelligence Services).

Where Pakistan, Lahore. A brothel bedroom used to entertain clients. It's squalid but tidy. A few Lollywood film posters on the wall. Also, a made bed, a CD player, clothes, make-up, cheap shoes. A stand fan spinning slowly, barely working.

When 2009. Evening.

What Has Just Happened Tariq has come in search of information about Mullah Hamid, rumoured to be one of Shaida's clients. Mullah Hamid is a terrorist leader whom Tariq mistakenly thinks he killed in action, an act for which Tariq has been highly commended by his superior officers.

Tariq Can I come in?

Shaida My begum isn't here, Saab.

Tariq I was told only one person lives here.

Shaida You were told wrong, Saab. There's me and my begum that live here and she's out. And I don't know when she'll be back.

Pause

Tariq I'm ... I'm ... look, please could you open the door just for a moment. I have something important to ask ...

She hides the notebook she had in the prologue. She opens the door.

Shaida You're supposed to talk to my friend next door first.

Tariq   Your friend?

Shaida   I mean, my brother.

Tariq   There are other places around here. I could go somewhere else.

She considers.

Shaida   It's 900 rupees, saab.

Tariq   That's fine.

Shaida   Ten minutes.

Tariq   OK.

She lets him in. He takes in the room.

Shaida   I'm not supposed to work like this.

Tariq   I don't want to get you into trouble.

Shaida   There's a system, an agreement between me and my –

Tariq   Brother.

Shaida   Yes. I think it's important to stick to an agreement once you've made it. Don't you, saab?

She holds her hand out. He opens his wallet.

Shaida   There isn't much time.

Tariq   This won't take long.

Shaida   It never does, saab.

She takes off her dupatta and folds it neatly. She makes to take off her shalwar but stops. He hasn't made a move, and he looks uncomfortable.

Shaida   If you're looking for something . . . unusual, saab, I can't help you. You can talk to my friend. He's very . . . knowledgeable. He can find just about anything a person needs in Lahore.

Pause

Or . . . Do you . . . do you need to talk, saab? Sometimes people like to just talk.

He nods

Shaida   OK. That'll be extra.

Tariq   Why?

Shaida   Because I'm not paid to listen. But if you pay me extra, I can listen.

Another 100 rupees.

He hands the money over.

Tariq   I have more.

Shaida   Lucky you, saab.

She sits down, waits. He's silent, but keeps looking around.

Tariq   You like to read.

He points to the Faiz poetry book from the prologue which she has forgotten to put away. She is thrown by this – this is private; the men don't get to know this about her.

Shaida   No, not really. Someone must have left it here.

Tariq   Who?

Shaida   I don't know.

Tariq   It's poetry. They like poetry, the . . . people who come –

Shaida   Yes. Maybe. Who doesn't love to be touched by beauty, by the poet's truth.

He laughs; he can't tell if she's serious or not.

Tariq   I'm not much of a reader, my wife . . . my wife thinks I hate art.

Shaida   Do you?

Tariq   No. I like to be entertained. I like films. I used to read as a boy. English books: *The Count of Monte Cristo, Treasure Island.* I enjoyed them.

Shaida   But –

Tariq   I wanted real adventures instead.

Shaida   Did you have any?

Tariq   Some. They don't always end as well as in the books.

Shaida   I can't read English. Are their writers as good as ours? There can't be anyone as good as Faiz, saab.

Tariq   They think theirs are the best in the world.

Shaida   How would they know if they haven't read Faiz?

Tariq   I think that *is* how they know.

Shaida   What else interests you, saab? Music, cricket?

Tariq   I don't get much time for –

Shaida   Family, then. You look like a family man, saab. You have children? Saab?

Tariq   Yes. I do.

Pause

Shaida   Many people who come here do. It's alright.

Tariq   I'm not here for –

Shaida   Friendship.

Tariq   I'm looking for . . . information on someone.

Shaida   Oh?

Tariq   I think you know him.

Pause.

Shaida   Are you a police officer, saab? Because we make our payments every week –

Tariq   I'm not –

Shaida   Well, you don't look like a debt collector. Or a gangster . . . sometimes they come looking for people . . . missing people.

Tariq   I'm not a debt collector –

Shaida   I'm new to the Mohalla. So –

Tariq   Hamid Mirza. I'm looking for information on Hamid Mirza. I heard you knew him.

Shaida   I don't know the name, saab.

Tariq   Mullah Hamid. Some people call him Mullah Hamid.

Shaida   Mullah Hamid?

Tariq   Yes.

Pause.

Shaida   Why would you want information on him, saab? He's dead. I saw it on the news. On Geo. There was an operation. There was a lot of *rolla* when they got him.

I think he was a big fish.

Tariq   I've heard he used to come here. That he . . . that you and he were friends.

Pause.

Shaida   Who are you, saab?

Tariq   Have you heard from him?

Shaida   I can't talk to the dead, saab.

Tariq   His people –

Shaida   But there is a baba just at the corner of the bazaar who says he can pass messages to the dead for only 30 rupees. My friend swears by him –

Tariq   I can have you arrested. If you don't tell me the truth.

Shaida   You said you weren't with the police.

Tariq   I'm not. I'm with the agencies.

Shaida *looks unsettled now.*

Shaida   I told you, saab. I don't know anything.

Tariq   Did he used to come here?

Shaida   No. I mean, I don't know. A lot of men come here.

Tariq   You'd know him. Mullah Hamid. Big beard. Big voice. Talks about infidels and djinns, likes to bomb mosques –

Shaida   They've all got beards these days, saab. You have a beard.

Tariq   Why would your name have come up? If he wasn't . . . or if other militants didn't come here?

Shaida   I don't know . . . I'm . . .

Tariq   Why have you been linked to him?

Shaida   I don't know. It doesn't cost much to come here to see me. 900 rupees isn't much. Some girls in the Mohalla charge in the thousands.

Tariq   Is this his? Did he like poetry? He liked to read to you after –

Shaida   I think time's up, saab.

Tariq   I have more money.

Shaida   I don't want any more money.

She holds her hand out for the book, but he doesn't hand it over.

Shaida   Please, saab. Please. Give it to me . . . Please, that's mine.

Tariq   You said someone left it.

Shaida   It's mine.

Tariq   You lied.

Shaida   No. Yes. I'm sorry, it's just –

Tariq   Should I talk to him? Your man, your friend, brother, next door.

Shaida   He's just an old baba, drunk most of the time. I just say it because . . . It . . . it helps if the men don't think I'm alone.

Tariq   You keep lying.

Shaida   I'm sorry, saab. I know it must look bad. But I don't know who comes to see me. I don't . . . I don't ask about them.

Tariq   I want the truth –

Shaida   I'm telling the –

Tariq   It's not good enough, not good enough. *Maa di.*

He throws the book down; his gesture is violent, frightening for her. She flinches.

Shaida   Please, saab. I want to help. I do. Please . . . don't hurt me.

Tariq   I'm not – look – I don't want to –

He sits down, overwhelmed.

Shaida   You don't look well, saab. Are you alright?

Tariq   No. I'm fine. It's hot in here. That's all.

Pause.

Shaida   The mullah's dead, saab. The army knows – they got him – there was a raid. A fire. It was on TV.

Tariq   . . .

Shaida   They don't make mistakes on the TV.

She looks uncertain now.

Do they?

Tariq   We know he used to come here.

Pause. She considers him.

Shaida   You really think he got away?

Tariq   That you know him.

Shaida   Because if that were true –

Tariq   I didn't say that.

Pause.

Shaida   Are you the only one who knows, saab?

Tariq   I need to –

Shaida   Find him? Yes? . . . Before he does something.

Tariq   No, that's not –

Shaida   Before anyone else finds out?

Pause.

I would tell you, saab, I would. If I knew, I would tell you.

Tariq   I can have you followed, I can have you arrested. I can make life hell for you.

Pause.

Shaida   I don't think you'll do that, saab. You don't seem . . . like an agency man.

Pause.

Tariq   Did he ever come here? I need to know.

Shaida   No. Maybe. I don't know.

Tariq   Please.

Shaida   That's the truth, saab . . . When they're here, I try . . . not to be. I try to think of other things, of other places, of anything. Sometimes of . . .

She picks up the poetry book

I don't talk to them. I hardly look at them. And when they're gone . . . I try to forget it all.

Tariq   . . .

Shaida   Just like this. Like you coming here. And the . . . things we've talked about.

You'll leave. And I'll forget you ever came. I'm always true to an agreement.

I wouldn't get you into any kind of trouble. Not with anyone.

The sound of the azaan.

Shaida   Asr. You know what that means, sahib?

Tariq   . . .

Shaida   Time's up.

First presented by Kali Theatre in March 2016 at Leicester Curve, Arcola Theatre and on tour.

Bitched

Sharon Raizada

Suzanne Fifty-one. Glamorous and rich, she runs her own interior design company and co-owns the fashionable art gallery Howl with her partner Nirjay. She has children: Mia, aged eight and Max, aged three. On the surface, Suzanne and Nirjay seem like they have the perfect life. But in reality, she's constantly picking up after Nirjay, who is irresponsible with money and she believes to be unfaithful.

Ali Thirty. A talented hair stylist and mother of Finn, aged two. Her partner, Rob, father of Finn, is a struggling, undiscovered artist and also a chef. Ali wants to progress her career, but Rob prefers her to be a stay-at-home mum. Ali is pressured and overworked, managing a part-time hairdressing job with low pay, whilst looking after Finn and supporting Rob's fledgling career as an artist.

Where London, Islington. Suzanne and Nirjay's huge living room.

When Present Day. Afternoon.

What Has Just Happened A week before this scene, Suzanne and Nirjay made an offer to Rob for his artwork, taking him on as one of Howl gallery's key artists. Rob accepted. Since then Rob and Nirjay have been spending their time bonding. Ali and Suzanne have met just once before at a Howl social gathering/networking event. They enter carrying a glass of wine.

Ali He's round Howl again.

Suzanne They're / 'bonding' –

Ali He's been pissed for a week.

Suzanne Young artists'd kill for it, believe me.

Ali Well, whatever it is, he can't hack it –
It's night of the living dead round ours every morning.

Suzanne   Poor little lambs . . . (*Tops them up.*) They should try giving birth.

Ali   Oh my God . . . (*Drinks.*) Did you feel shocked? . . . Like body shock? I mean that was *extreme* . . .

Suzanne   C-section. All booked in. Didn't feel a thing –

Ali   *Really?* . . . I mean, that last bit where he got stuck and they pulled him out –

Suzanne   Maybe too much information –

Ali   . . . flashbacks . . . and . . . *wounds / Christ* –

Suzanne   Honey, take the drugs.

Ali   And afterwards . . . it's like your nerves are slashed . . . Did you find / that?

Suzanne   You get a morphine drip, button. They leave you to it.

Ali   Like you've been in a *car crash* or something . . . and crawled out the wreckage.

Suzanne   The NHS as dealer.

Ali   And sex was like that, at first. . . . Was it for you?

Suzanne   Well, I was intact. Just had to watch the scab.

Ali   It was like . . . there's something going on . . . but it's *miles* away, like someone waving a light at the end of a tunnel.

Suzanne   The French get it right. No breastfeeding to stop them dropping. Prescribed PC exercise and copious use of sex toys to get you back in shape.

Ali   . . . And their men totally cheat on them.

Suzanne   Everyone cheats.

Ali   Don't know how they have the energy.

Suzanne   Though sex generally stops once you're married –

Beat.

Makes everyone more uptight.

Ali (*embarrassed*)   It's a beautiful space! I . . . love the walls.

Suzanne   It's what I do.

Ali   Which is what, exactly?

Suzanne   I decorate. Personal, client-led schemes. Classic design with a twist.

Ali   You run a company?

Suzanne   I run myself.

Ali   You run that *and* the gallery?

Suzanne   Not really, Nirjay's baby. I'm non-executive director.

Ali   What's that mean?

Suzanne   I keep them afloat.

Ali   . . . So, why 'Howl'?

Suzanne   Nirjay's hobby horse . . . And for God's sake don't ask him, he'll start quoting Ginsberg –

Ali   You sound like you don't like him very much.

Suzanne   Men, honey, are either arseholes or sweethearts. But with an arsehole I know what I'm looking at.

Ali   Don't you love him?

Suzanne   Do you love yours?

Ali   Of / course.

Suzanne   It's the marriage myth. We're at our sexual peak in our forties, men at eighteen. It's us should be trading in for a younger model . . . Or one with tits.

Ali   By their forties most men have tits.

Suzanne   Does Robert?

Ali   No.

Suzanne   Good for you. Nirjay would if I didn't shame him in public.

Ali   Is that nice?

Suzanne   It's what they do to us. (*Tops them up.*) Though divorce I can get behind.

Ali   . . . (*Glances at her.*) Oh my God . . .

Suzanne   All my divorced friends have the best lives.

(*Considers.*) All that time and money and freedom.

Ali   Is Rob going to make any money? At the show?

Suzanne   . . . He'll sell I'm sure. . . . But if it's down to Nirj . . . overheads, expenses . . . I hate to say it –

Ali (*tight*)   What do you mean?

Suzanne   He's a useless bastard with cash.

Ali   Don't say that! *We need it.*

She stops.

Suzanne   Well, in that case, I shall oversee it – as a personal favour. I'll do the accounts.

Ali   *Thank you* . . . thank you. Anything to help. So why are you with him, if that's what you think?

Suzanne   Because he's a dad, they do dad things . . . It's important for Max. My dad wasn't . . . a home body. We're all on What'sApp, it's really quite convenient –

Ali   You think it's worth it for Max?

Suzanne   Honey, a child is worth ten men.

Ali   That's harsh.

Suzanne   You / think?

Ali   I gotta get Finn.

Suzanne (*changes tack*)   That job. You go for it?

Ali   Yeah . . . (*Rises.*) I didn't get it.

Suzanne   Well done though –

Ali   They didn't want me.

Suzanne   But you dipped your toe in the water, honey. . . . Baby steps . . . it's a process.

Ali   . . . It felt good you know. Good to be back –

Suzanne   I'm sure.

Ali   I *was good.*

Suzanne   You *are good, honey*. Never forget it – (*Drinks.*) Never give up your earning power, or you're screwed. Don't give in to kiddie oblivion –

Ali   *Kiddie oblivion?*

Suzanne   Rat race too much? Give it up . . . have a kid! Have three, four . . . why stop there?

Ali   It's not giving up! *It's making a family.*

Suzanne *looks at her.*

Suzanne   Women are bred to please others and men to please themselves. Fact of life.

Ali   Rob's not like that.

Suzanne   And after kids, we're a nag, a scold. They don't see us anymore.

Ali   . . . (*Reluctant.*) I hate those words.

Suzanne   It's the seven ages of woman: babe, sulk, slag, bitch, scold, harridan, hag. Unless we *fight*.

Ali   Fight?

Suzanne   Stop wanting to be liked for goodness' sake! Men follow their desires and they're strong. Don't be defined by them not / us –

Ali   I won't be defined by / anyone.

Suzanne   How often do you have sex?

Ali   . . . *Excuse me?*

Suzanne   You brought it up . . .

Ali   How often do *you*?

Suzanne   Well, Max was a miracle, could have been the immaculate conception – Though pregnancy was better, he loves pregnant woman.

Ali   . . . (*Confesses.*) I had to beg Rob to have sex when I was pregnant, I was nearly in tears.

Suzanne   All that horn and nowhere to put it.

Ali   We're trying for another.

Suzanne (*forces herself*)   . . . That's . . . wonderful news –

Ali   Not *kiddie oblivion*?

Suzanne (*makes a visible effort*)   . . . I'm delighted for you.

She gulps wine, refills their glasses.

Ali (*leaving*)   Gonna be too pissed for pick-up –

Suzanne (*turns, brightly*)   Both! You should *do both*. / Of course –

Ali   Both?

Suzanne   Set up on your own, if you're good. *And* try –

Why limit / yourself?

Ali   I am good.

Suzanne   Hairdressing's recession proof, the perfect mobile business –

Keep costs down, profits up . . . sky's the limit.

Ali   Oh my God, my mate did that! He's got this amazing salon now, he started from home –

Suzanne   There / you go.

Ali   Why didn't I think of this before? He can give me some advice!

Suzanne   And whatever grows *is meant to be* . . .

Ali   Thank you, thank you – (*Reaches for mobile.*) I could kiss you!

Suzanne *watches* Ali, *who's texting.*

Suzanne   All part of the service –

She's unreadable.

First presented by Kali Theatre in October 2017 at Tristan Bates Theatre.

Noor

Azma Dar

Noor (Inayat Khan; also known as Madeleine.)   Late twenties. Dual heritage – Indian/American. Brought up in Paris and London. Sufi Muslim, musician, writer and Second World War British spy. Noor was the first female radio operator to be dropped behind enemy lines in Occupied France. She was eventually betrayed and captured, and died in Dachau concentration camp in 1944. She was posthumously awarded the George Cross, Britain's highest civilian honour.

Kieffer (Major Hans)   Early forties. German and a high-ranking member of the Nazi Party. Married with children.

Where   Occupied France. Paris. Kieffer's office.

When   Second World War. 1942. Evening.

What Has Just Happened   Noor has been imprisoned by Kieffer after evading capture for around three months. Fascinated by her, Kieffer has sent an evening dress to her cell and requested that she join him for dinner. Kieffer is laying a table with plates, glasses, cutlery, flowers, candles, food. He lights the candles and puts on some music (Bach). Noor enters wearing the dress and a little make-up.

NB: Both Noor and Kieffer were real people and the play is based on research into their lives.

Kieffer   My goodness! I did not recognise you, Madeleine!

He pulls out a chair. They sit.

I hope you don't mind me calling you that? It's the name I've become most familiar with, after hunting you all this time.

He laughs.

Noor   What's so funny?

Kieffer   You're no longer the cat that pounced on me. Your attack was vicious but I couldn't help admiring your wildness, your courage.

Beat.

You look beautiful.

Noor   If you think flattery will get you more information, you're wrong.

Kieffer   Thank you for your previous information. It was completely useless, as you well knew. Trains going south.

Noor   I thought I'd keep you busy.

Kieffer   You play an interesting game, Madeleine.

Beat.

But tonight I would like something else. I don't want to know about spies and secrets.

Noor   What else do I have?

Kieffer   I just want you to talk to me. About yourself and what makes you happy.

Noor   Why?

Kieffer   Because . . . I am in need of the company. Even I get tired of all this.

I will forget it all when I leave this room.

Noor   What do you want to know?

Kieffer   It is your choice. Perhaps . . . what do you enjoy when you are just a normal girl? Do you like music? I enjoy Bach when I have the moment to myself.

Noor   When are you going to torture me?

Kieffer   What? Do you think if I was going to torture you I would go to all this trouble? You must think I am the most twisted individual.

Noor   I've been expecting it since I came here, bracing myself for it.

Kieffer   There will be nothing of that sort while you are in my care.

Pause.

Noor   I love Bach. I play too. I mean . . .

Kieffer   A musician? What do you play?

Noor   The harp, mostly, and the piano.

Kieffer   You like writing too, I think.

Noor   How do you know that?

Kieffer   You are always asking for paper.

Noor   Oh. I wrote a book . . . for children. It's called . . . I shouldn't say.

Kieffer   Can I read it? I tell my children stories when I can.

Noor   Perhaps, when it's finished. I don't like showing people unfinished work.

Kieffer   I admire people who are able to create beauty. I could never do it myself.

Noor   Beauty's everywhere. You just have to notice it. Seek it out.

Kieffer   What? Here, in this prison, amongst cages and chains? You have a strange idea of the aesthetic. This is a place of terror, deception, the dirtiest of human emotions.

Noor   There, look at that.

Kieffer   It's a barred window. I would say one of the ugliest things in the world, even to me.

Noor   Beyond that. Through it.

Kieffer   There is nothing except a sliver of moon.

Noor   A gleaming silver crescent on a deep velvet sky

Pause.

Kieffer   It might ease my mind to look at the sky instead of staring at these dreary maps all the time. I will remember you. This moment.

Beat.

You're a woman of culture, taste. Sensibilities. I've never seen anyone like you in a place like this before.

Noor   I do love those things . . . music and poetry . . . but what use are they if we aren't free?

Pause.

Kieffer   I picked the dress myself, you know, to suit you. And I was right. It is perfect. Look how it glides over your shoulders and brings out the darkness of your eyes.

Pause.

Noor   If you love beauty so much, why are you doing all of this?

Kieffer   Beauty is recreation. The rest is work.

Beat.

Noor   Why do you hate the Jewish people? Do you really think you're superior?

Kieffer   Are you Jewish? No – don't answer that.

Beat.

I admit, for some the 'supremacy' idea has become an obsession. But for me, it is more the other issues. There are some troublemakers among them, you know. Traitors. They cost us the last war.

Noor   You can't hold an entire race to account for the action of a few.

Kieffer   Even if I agree with you I'm powerless to prevent it.

Noor   It only takes one man to make a stand, to inspire others.

Kieffer   That, I do believe. We are seeing it every day with our own eyes.

Noor   Then why not you? You can start to make things right again.

Pause.

Kieffer   How?

Noor   You could stop arresting people.

Kieffer   Yes, I could 'go easy' on the arrests for a few weeks. I could even stop playing my radio game.

Pause.

Do you really think I would betray the land of my ancestors?

Noor   We don't owe everything to our ancestors. If I believed that I wouldn't be here.

Kieffer   Well, for me it is the important thing. Our country was destroyed but we have built the strong new nation. We have social and economic stability once more.

Noor   Don't you think nations work better together, for peaceful solutions, instead of being isolated?

Kieffer   Yes, we can work with others. As long as we are in control, have more power than anyone else.

Noor   We won't let it happen. Can't you see it's a deluded belief?

Kieffer   Oh, Madeleine, I'm really just an ordinary man who wants a safe future for his children. Sometimes I think what if we lose? What will become of them?

Beat.

But I can't talk like this. It's a crime to even have doubts. A crime to think differently, behave differently in these black times. Even be born different. You'll do well to remember that.

Noor   I can't change what I am.

Kieffer   Then don't draw attention. Become a bystander, Madeleine, not the main attraction.

Pause.

I have the things you asked for.

He hands her a package.

Noor   Thank you. I appreciate your kindness.

Kieffer   Don't trust anyone, Madeleine. Especially not me. Never forget that I am the enemy.

Noor was presented by Kali as part of the War Plays Festival in May 2018 at Tristan Bates Theatre. It is currently being developed for a full production.

Sundowning

Nessah Muthy

Teresa   Late thirties. Working class from Surrey. Betty's daughter. Alyssa's aunt.

Alyssa   Early twenties. Mixed race. Working class from Surrey. Grand-daughter of Betty who has brought her up and with whom she has had a very close and loving relationship. Teresa's only niece.

Where   Outside the front door of Betty's house (the family home), Tadworth, Surrey (not the posh part, the council estate) where Teresa currently lives but is selling up to pay for Betty's care.

When   Present day. December. Evening.

What Has Just Happened   Betty has Alzheimer's disease. She is now in a care home. Teresa has been her sole carer while Alyssa has been in prison sentenced with fraud. (Alyssa's plumbing business went bankrupt and she tried to pay off her debts with Betty's credit card.) Alyssa has now been released and has returned straight back to the family home, without knowing any of the latest news. This is the opening scene of the play.

Darkness.
A fairy light spits on. Off. On.
Silence.

Alyssa   How? How . . . er . . . how . . . is. . . . is she?

Teresa   No –

Alyssa   No . . .?

Beat.

Alyssa   You, selling? Selling up?

Beat.

Where you going?

Beat.

Eh?! Where you taking her?

Beat.

Teresa   There's a smell.

Beat.

It's you. You stink.

Alyssa   I ran here –

Teresa   Shit.

Alyssa   Sweat.

Teresa   Shit.

Alyssa   Sweat sometimes smells like shit –

Teresa   No it doesn't.

Alyssa   A little, mine, mine does –

Teresa   Shat yourself? You always used to. When you got scared. Are you scared?

Are you?

Beat.

Maybe it's not you. Maybe it's her.

Alyssa   I'd like to see her –?

Teresa   Would you?

Alyssa   Yes.

Teresa   You're sure?

Alyssa   Yes –

Teresa   Whatever you're imagining, it's worse. Much, much worse –

Alyssa   Please.

Beat.

Please –

Teresa   No. I've put her to bed –

Alyssa It's early –

Teresa It's late –

Alyssa It's –

Teresa Bedtime.

Alyssa Tomorrow?

Beat.

I'll come back. Any time.

Beat.

Any time you say.

Beat.

Alyssa Please.

Beat.

Just a little while, just . . .

Beat.

I'm here now. I can help –

Teresa Oh . . .?

Alyssa Yeah –

Teresa Right –

Alyssa Yes.

Teresa You're here now . . .

Beat.

Feel them –

Alyssa What –?

Teresa Feel my hands. Feel them –

Alyssa What? What are you doing?! Stop it. Get off –

Teresa Like a fucking cheese grater –

Alyssa Stop. Stop it!

Beat.

Teresa   She's mine.

Beat.

Oh . . . nasty, who'd you piss off . . . nasty new face . . . scratched right up . . . what'd you do in there eh? Eh –?

Alyssa   I just want to tell her, I want to tell her . . . I think about her all the time . . . I can't stop thinking about her . . . I –

Teresa   She hasn't got any money –

Alyssa   No, I didn't, no, I'm not –

Teresa   There isn't any left –

Alyssa   I don't –

Teresa   Liar –

Alyssa   I don't want any fucking money alright?! I've got me fucking forty quid . . . and me tent . . .

Teresa   What?!

Alyssa   That's what you get. None of this . . . it wasn't ever about, about –

Teresa   Thieving –

Alyssa   No –

Teresa   Selfish –

Beat.

Alyssa   I was, I was gonna rescue them, they, they were gonna be proud . . .

Beat.

Alyssa   I'm sorry.

Beat.

I wanna, I wanna tell her, please . . .

Beat.

She'd want to see me.

Beat.

I'm telling you, she'd want to. You know she would.

Beat.

I need to see –

Teresa   I'm giving you a warning –

Alyssa   Don't –

Teresa   Now.

Alyssa   LET ME SEE HER!

Teresa   Gonna go in there, like this, like a fucking monster are you, are you –?

Alyssa *scoffs, snorts.*

Teresa   After I've rocked her to sleep like a baby.

Silence.

Alyssa *leaves.*

Silence.

Alyssa *returns.*

Alyssa   How is she?

Beat.

Just . . .

Beat.

Alyssa   Please . . .

Beat.

Alyssa   Is . . . Is . . . she's –?

Teresa   Yes, yes she's dead.

Alyssa   What?

Teresa   Yes –

Alyssa   What?!

Teresa   Yes –

Alyssa   She's . . .

Teresa   Yes –

Alyssa   Is she? Is she?

Teresa   She's dead, yes.

Silence.

Alyssa *sobs.*

Silence.

You let me; you let me stand there and . . . you let me . . . you let me . . .

She sobs.

Silence.

When?!

Beat.

How?

Beat.

Where's . . . Where is she?

Beat.

Was she buried?

Beat.

Teresa   I –

Beat.

I, I don't know –

Alyssa   Did you burn her? She didn't want to be burnt, did you burn her?!

Beat.

Where is she?!

Teresa   I don't know –

Alyssa   You don't know!?

Teresa   No –

Alyssa   How can you not, how can you not fucking (know) – ?!

Teresa   I'm going to call the police now.

Alyssa   Tell me!

Beat.

TELL ME NOW!

Silence.

Teresa   Stay away; stay far, far away from us.

Alyssa   She's not is she?

Teresa   Go –

Alyssa   Tell me she's not?!

Teresa   She's not –

Alyssa   She's not?

Beat.

Where is she?!

Beat.

I'll find her –

Teresa   She's dead, she's gone –

Alyssa   What – ?!

Teresa   She's gone –

Alyssa   Why are you doing this?! WHY?!

Teresa   Don't, don't please, please, don't hurt –

Alyssa   I wasn't going to . . .

Silence.

Teresa *sobs.*

Teresa   I've put her away. I've had to send her away . . .

Alyssa   I'll find her.

Beat.

I will.

First presented by Kali Theatre in October 2018 at Plymouth Drum, Tristan Bates Theatre and on tour.

Homing Birds

Rukhsana Ahmad

Saeed Mid-twenties. Afghan. Fled Afghanistan as a child refugee.
Adopted by a UK family (Michael and Jenny). Recently returned to
Kabul as a newly qualified UK doctor to work with MSF (Médecins
Sans Frontières). Saeed is searching for his lost sister, Nazneen. He
suffers from PTSD (post-traumatic stress disorder).

Raabia Late thirties. Afghan minister responsible for women. Clever,
driven, charismatic, ambitious. Married to Mustafa. Raabia has had many
attempts on her life by right wing extremists.

Where Raabia's heavily guarded, elegant home in central Kabul.

When Present time. Morning.

What has just happened Saeed previously met Raabia at a charity
event in London where she inspired and encouraged him to return to
Afghanistan (against his adoptive father's wishes). Raabia is desperate to
rebuild the country and lure young Afghan talent back to help with that.
Saeed is possessed by his dream of reuniting with his sister Nazneen,
who might be alive and close by somewhere in Kabul. He has lived with
constant flashbacks of their early childhood together. This is his second
meeting with Raabia.

Saeed Amazing house, Mrs. Durrani. The security arrangements are
watertight.

Didn't think I'd get in /

Raabia Hope the guards didn't hassle you?

Saeed Not at all. It's all necessary.

Raabia Sadly, yes! Before we sit down . . . Mustafa, my husband, is
sorry he can't join us. A slipped disc, I'm afraid! Now . . . green tea,
black tea or something cold?

Saeed I'm exhausted. A good coffee to keep me awake. Or English
breakfast tea, please.

Raabia   I like a tinge of the flag in mine. Green – that's my normal order at this time of day.

She rings bell.

Saeed   Nothing to beat our green tea.

Raabia   That's the spirit, Saeed. Afghanistan is a very special place.

Saeed   I believe in it, totally. Even argued with Michael, at times. But soon as I came off the plane, they got to me. I kept thinking: 'Noisy, disorderly brutes. No one's willing to queue, or wait their turn.' Even cars, buses, carts ran higgledy piggledy on the road to the Babur Garden – and that was a big disappointment on my very first day!

Raabia   What? You did the Bagh-e-Babur on your first day in Kabul? A serious tourist, aren't you?

Saeed   Awful, to become a tourist in your motherland! No? It's the only chance I got. The hospital's full-on!

Raabia   Glad you made it to the gardens, even if you didn't like them.

Saeed   Wasn't the gardens I went for – I went looking for my family.

Raabia   Did they live round there?

Saeed   I think so. I wondered if you might be able to help? Been trying for a month to find them. I've found no clues at all.

Raabia   For sure. I'll help – all I can . . .

Saeed   It was a shock to see the place. The American University is where our homes used to be. I couldn't imagine the end of an entire community. Gone. All of them! I expected to find a few leads, some people from the past. I found none at all.

Raabia   Decimated. In thirty years of war we've lost millions of lives, thousands of homes, hundreds of villages . . .

Saeed   Doesn't the government keep records? Of compensation schemes, for example?

Raabia   People died, people fled, or were driven away. No one could maintain records back then. This war is older than you, Saeed.

Saeed   Even so.

Raabia   When the Allied Forces got here, they were terrified of anyone in a turban. They bombed areas suspected of protecting militants until they were routed. And the Taliban mined every inch of land they surrendered. Destroyed communities.

Saeed   Moray was alone the day our house was hit. Is there any hope of finding my sister?

Raabia   There's always hope. The future is bursting with promise. (*Beat.*) You're here now, Saeed! That's a good start.

Saeed   Where do I begin to look?

Raabia   Let me have full names and addresses . . .

Saeed   I've one sibling who survived the invasion. Nazneen, my sister. She was married off. But I've no contact details for her /

Raabia   Not even her husband's name?

Saeed   Baba told me on the phone, but I'm afraid I forgot.

Raabia   Tough. But don't worry. We'll find a way to trace her . . . First, tell me, which hospital did you join?

Saeed   The MSF Hospital in the South. Thank you so much for getting me to Kabul. I felt the pull of helpful strings.

Raabia   Don't mention it. Enjoying working with them I hope?

Saeed   Immensely! A fine team of dedicated doctors and staff. Ever ready to improvise and make do! Huge learning curve for me. Do come and meet them. You'll see why I think they're terrific.

Raabia   I'd love to. Thanks. Might make a good photo op for us?

Saeed   I'm talking to an Afghan computer geek from the US. We're building a database to link our doctors digitally to consultants in the UK – to talk them through latest treatments. I'll match up the right specialist for each case /

Raabia   Not many British doctors come out here. They're too nervous.

Saeed   I can incentivise them to advise doctors here remotely about complex cases on Skype, WhatsApp, Viber, whatever.

Raabia   Fantastic! I knew you'd be worth your weight in gold – you've proved my point. So important to get our young talent back.

Saeed   Thanks for having faith in me. All hypothetical so far.

Raabia   It's a great idea. I can make it happen. Times are tough but we might even get some US sponsorship. Right?

Saeed   I don't know about funding or resources. I'm a worker in a white coat. Give me patients and I'll get them well again . . .

Raabia   Great soundbite. You're so quotable, Saeed. I'll get our press office to profile this issue here and in the UK and this idea will become reality long before you return to England . . .

Saeed   If only I wanted to be a celebrity! But all I want is peace and order in my life and a happy ending to my search.

Raabia   I understand your need to connect with family. I'll help, I swear. But we need young Afghans to come back here and team up with those of us who are ready to pull out into the twenty-first century.

Saeed   Careful what you wish for. There are all sorts in the diaspora: not everyone who lives overseas is liberal or liberated.

Raabia   Good point. Tell me what you think of Kabul now?

Saeed   The MSF team are committed to the hilt. But we've no infrastructure, no organisational support. And I hate seeing under-age pregnancies. One of our counsellors wants to campaign against child marriages. I knew you'd help her so I promised I'd request you to take her under your wing.

Raabia   Early marriages? A tough one. She has the right idea – it's a major, major issue for women. But, as a nation, the one we need to focus on right now is the economy.

Saeed   I'm so sorry. I've already told her you'd support the cause.

Raabia   I do, of course I do. I agree it's the biggest obstacle to women's education, health and survival. But we've got to work out a strategy, a pitch, to avoid a backlash.

Saeed   Well, then, I probably raised her hopes too high. Will you please, at least, see her?

Raabia   Of course I will – also, I hope and pray we find your sister soon.

Saeed   Counting on you, Mrs Durrani. I'm not good at prayers but I wish you the best.

Exit **Saeed**.

She lights a candle. Uses it to light another two.

Raabia   I was the seventh daughter. My mother got no flowers, no gifts, no thanks for giving birth to me. Instead, she got a divorce. Until I was ten, she dressed me like a boy – our neighbours thought I was a boy. It hid her shame and it protected me – but that also made me feel stronger inside. I can tap that strength to fight for Afghan women.

The day I turned fourteen, a palmist at the school fair predicted I'd get married before the year was out. Never, I told her. I'll make it to the highest office. I'm going to university. (*Beat.*) That might happen too, she said calmly.

And it came to pass, just so. Mustafa saw me at my father's funeral and proposed. I agreed to marry him before I was fifteen, but only if he promised he'd help me get a degree. He kept his word, let me realise my dreams. He's my sponsor, the father of my children, my mentor and my lover, all rolled into one. Raabia jan, he said, the Americans are kinder to Afghan women than their own. They've reserved half the seats in our parliament for women . . . success will come easier to you than me. And he was right. I'm on my way, Madar-jaan. One final hurdle and I shall make it.

This woman at the hospital is right – child marriages are a key issue. What if I break the taboo and speak out against them? I'll work on Mustafa and get him to see it my way. 'It's that final leap I need, Jaanum, to get women's votes Don't you see?'

First presented by Kali Theatre in October 2019 at Plymouth Drum, Tara Theatre and on tour.

Writer Biographies

Rukhsana Ahmad

Stage plays include: *River on Fire* (finalist, Susan Smith Blackburn International Award), *Letting Go, Mistaken, Homing Birds*. For the BBC: originals, adaptations and a screenplay. *Wide Sargasso Sea* (finalist, Writers' Guild Award Best Radio Adaptation); *Song for a Sanctuary* (finalist CRE Award, Best Original Radio Drama), *Maps for Lost Lovers* (adapted from Nadeem Aslam's novel) (UKFC and Keel Films). www.rukhsanaahmad.com

Naylah Ahmed

Naylah writes for theatre, radio and TV. Her stage plays include: *Butcher Boys* (Bruntwood Prize 2008); *Mustafa* (Birmingham Rep/Kali); *Ready or Not* (Kali); *When the Fire's Gone Out* (Kali Home Festival); *A Christmas Carol* adaptation (Jermyn Street Theatre/Guildford Shakespeare Company 2020). She is a core writer on *The Archers*.

Aamina Ahmad

Aamina was born and raised in London. Her play *The Dishonoured* was produced by Kali and toured the UK in 2016. The play won the 2019 Screencraft Stage Play Award. She holds an MFA in fiction from the Iowa Writers' Workshop. Her first novel is forthcoming from Riverhead in 2022.

Miriam Babooram

Miriam was a member of Kali's TalkBack Program in 2016. Since then she has written several short plays and monologues, including *Hair* which premiered at the Arts Theatre, London as part of *Female Edit:100* and has recently been recorded as an audio drama for Ragged Foils Isolation Sessions.

Alia Bano

Alia is an Evening Standard and Critics' Circle Award-winning playwright. Her plays include: *Shades* (Royal Court Theatre); *Hens* (SkyArtsLive); *Parwana* (Wexner Centre, Ohio). She has written for children's TV and is working on original TV material.

Sonali Bhattacharyya

Sonali's plays include: *Megaball* (National Theatre Learning); *Slummers* (Cardboard Citizens); *The Invisible Boy* (Kiln); *2066* (Almeida); *Deepa the Saint* (Women's Prize for Playwriting shortlist); *Chasing Hares* (Nick Darke Prize shortlist and Sonia Friedman Production Award winner). Current commissions: Fifth Word and Kiln Theatre. Writer in residence at National Theatre Studio. www.sonaliwrites.com

Sharmila Chauhan

Sharmila's work is often a transgressive meditation on love, sexuality and the diasporic experience. Her plays, including *The Husbands*, *Born Again/ Purnajanam* and *Be Better in Bed*, all place women centre stage and explore power and femininity. Sharmila has had two short films (*Girl Like You and Oysters*) produced and is working on her debut screenplay. www. SharmilaTheWriter.com

Satinder Chohan

Hailing from Southall, West London, Satinder's plays include: *Zameen* (Kali Theatre UK tour); *KabaddiKabaddiKabaddi* (Pursued by a Bear/ Kali tour); *Made in India* (Tamasha Theatre UK tour); *Half of Me* (Lyric Hammersmith); and *Lotus Beauty* (Hampstead Theatre). Audio dramas include *Garlands* (BBC Radio 3), *Steam Rises* (Tamasha/National Archives) and *Girl of Ink and Stars* (Spark Arts).

Azma Dar

Azma's work includes plays *Chaos* and *Paper Thin*, radio play *The Escape* and short film *Reversion*. Her novel *The Secret Arts* was published as an e-book. An extract from *The Secret Arts* won the New Writing Ventures Award, and her play *Vampire in Bradford* won the New Perspectives play Competition.

Veronica J. Dewan

Veronica is of Irish and Indian descent. She was adopted and raised in England. Writing includes: *She Is Not Herself* (Kali Theatre); *Come to Where I'm From* (Paines Plough); *Mona's Garden* (Wiltshire Creative/All the Queens Men); *The Half Daughter* (BBC Upload/Radio Wiltshire). Plays in development: *Aftercare, Bustard* and *Papa India*.

Bettina Gracias

Bettina has had eleven plays produced by BBC Radio 4, one series on Radio Berkshire and two stage plays produced by Kali Theatre. She has won several awards for her writing. She has directed a short film which won best Web Film at the Druka Film Festival in Bhutan.

Emteaz Hussain

Emteaz's produced works include *Blood, Outsiders, Sweet Cider* and *Etching* for BBC Three, and more recently an adaptation of Alex Wheatle's *Crongton Knights*. She is currently commissioned by the Royal Court Theatre, London, for a new play *Erasure* and is a contributor to their The Living Newspaper writer collective.

Sayan Kent

Sayan is a playwright, librettist and composer. Her plays have been performed all over the country. She has been nominated for the John Whiting Award, shortlisted for the Terrence Rattigan Award, longlisted for the Bruntwood Prize and the Papatango Prize, and was joint winner of the Capital New Writing Festival.

Anu Kumar Lazarus

Anu's work includes: *Waterfall* (Ashfield Theatre); *The Ecstacy* (Kali/Ovalhouse), *Twelve* (Kali/Rich Mix); *Freedom* (Kali/Tristan Bates). Devising and collaborations: *Operation Black Antler* (Blast Theory); *Everything That Rises Must Dance* (Complicite); *The Filibuster Project* (Somerset House). Anu is a practising Hackney GP. www.sensorinet.com

Sonia Likhari

Sonia's first play, *Behna*, was developed for Kali's *Giving Voice* (Soho Theatre) and revived twice as a site-specific production with Birmingham Rep/Black Country Touring. Sonia was Artist in Residence with Tamasha Theatre (2007/8) and has written for Rifco Arts (*Where's My Desi Soulmate?*) Birmingham Rep (*Bazaar*), the BBC (*Silver Street, Snapshots, Resolutions, Ek Awaaz*) and CBBC (*Planet Ajay*).

Amber Lone

Amber is a writer from Birmingham, completing her MA in Creative Writing at Birkbeck. She has written for theatre and radio and is currently developing a short film and editing her first novel as well as embarking on writing for television.

Nessah Muthy

Nessah is a multi-award-winning, two times Writers' Guild-nominated, writer for stage and screen. She has worked with a number of leading theatres and arts organisations including the Royal Court Theatre, Punchdrunk, National Youth Theatre, Cardboard Citizens, HighTide, Kali Theatre, Theatre Centre, Iris Theatre, Cloakroom Theatre, King's Head Theatre and Gate Theatre/Royal Welsh College of Music and Drama.

Iman Qureshi

Iman is an award-winning writer for stage, screen and radio. In 2018 she won the Papatango New Writing Prize with her breakout play *The Funeral Director* which premiered at the Southwark Playhouse before a UK tour. She is currently working on a number of commissions for TV and theatre.

Sharon Raizada

Sharon is a writer, script editor and teacher. Her plays include *Bitched* (Tristan Bates Theatre); *Black i* (Ovalhouse); *Lady Play* (BBC Radio 4). Her work for screen includes *Apple Tree House* (CBeebies), *Emmerdale* (ITV) and award-winning shorts.

Atiha Sen Gupta

Atiha is a playwright and screenwriter. Her plays have been performed in Britain, Germany and Denmark. For TV, she has written for *Skins*, *Holby City* and *EastEnders*. She is interested in telling the stories of those who stitch the red carpet rather than those who stand on it.

Shelley Silas

Shelley's theatre plays include: *Eating Ice Cream on Gaza Beach* (NYT/Soho Theatre); *Falling* (Bush); *Calcutta Kosher* (Kali/Southwark Playhouse, Theatre Royal Stratford East, Arcola); *Mercy Fine* (Clean Break). Radio plays include *The Trial of the Well of Loneliness*, two series in Val McDermid's comedy crime *Dead* series and *I Am Emma Humphreys*.

Yasmin Whittaker-Khan

Yasmin is a writer, television presenter, producer and youth worker. Her plays have been translated and performed around the world, and her work has been broadcast by the BBC and Anglia Television. She has written for publications including *Index on Censorship*, *English Pen*, *Woman's Own* and the *Mail on Sunday*, and is the founder of Insaan Culture Club.